PRAISE FOR
FAT GIRLS IN BLACK BODIES

"*Fat Girls in Black Bodies* is essential reading for anyone interested in body liberation. Weaving together memoir and scholarship, Joy Cox shines a light on the intersecting oppressions faced by fat Black womxn in contemporary culture, and the power of community to help heal the wounds of injustice. I'm grateful to have this important book informing my work as a Health at Every Size healthcare provider and activist."

—CHRISTY HARRISON, MPH, RD, CDN, author of *Anti-Diet*

"For my fat Black sisters who have ever felt invisible or been mistreated by the world, or even your own people, you will find both healing and inspiration in this book. Joy Cox speaks to the complexity of our pain while reminding us of the vastness of our power. By sharing her wisdom, insight, and lived experience, she delivers a compelling charge for fat Black women to reclaim our personal autonomy and actualize social and communal change that will bring about liberation for us all."

—IVY FELICIA, The Body Relationship Coach™, founder of Fat Women of Color™

"*Fat Girls in Black Bodies* is a must-read for fat Black girls and those who seek to uplift our humanity in a sizeist, racist, and sexist society. Both a love letter and a call to action, Joy brilliantly weaves together the latest research, pop culture, and personal narratives of some of the most radical fat Black influencers, healers, entrepreneurs, academics, and activists, herself included. I laughed, I cried, and I felt seen. I'm honored to be mentioned in this work and cannot wait to share it with the world!"

—MAKIA GREEN, creator of Dear Fat Girls

"There is an enduring myth, especially amongst non-Black body positivity advocates, that fat Black women are somehow immune to the impacts of anti-fat stigma. Dr. Joy Cox knows better. Her examination of fatphobia within the Black community, as well as her insights on the cumulative impact of the stress of dealing with that in-community bias while also enduring external judgment on top of racism and sexism, is an important contribution to the dialogue on body liberation. The inclusion of additional voices from her popular podcast adds to the richness of this debut. I look forward to so much more from Dr. Joy."

—TIGRESS OSBORN, NAAFA Director of
Community Outreach and Co-Founder of
PHX Fat Force

Fat Girls in Black Bodies

Fat Girls in
Black Bodies

Creating Communities
of Our Own

JOY ARLENE RENEE COX, PHD

North Atlantic Books
Berkeley, California

Published by   Cover design by Jasmine Hromjak
North Atlantic Books   Book design by Happenstance Type-O-Rama
Berkeley, California

Printed in Canada

Fat Girls in Black Bodies: Creating Communities of Our Own is sponsored and published by the Society for the Study of Native Arts and Sciences (dba North Atlantic Books), an educational nonprofit based in Berkeley, California, that collaborates with partners to develop cross-cultural perspectives, nurture holistic views of art, science, the humanities, and healing, and seed personal and global transformation by publishing work on the relationship of body, spirit, and nature.

North Atlantic Books' publications are available through most bookstores. For further information, visit our website at www.northatlanticbooks.com or call 800-733-3000.

Library of Congress Cataloging-in-Publication Data
Names: Cox, Joy, author.
Title: Fat girls in black bodies : creating communities of our own / Joy Arlene Renee Cox, PhD.
Description: Berkeley, California : North Atlantic Books, [2020] | Includes bibliographical references and index. | Summary: "Combatting fatphobia and racism to reclaim a space of belonging at the intersection of fat, Black, and female."— Provided by publisher.
Identifiers: LCCN 2020006712 | ISBN 9781623174996 (trade paperback)
Subjects: LCSH: Cox, Joy. | Overweight women—United States—Biography. | African American women—Biography. | Obesity in women—Social aspects—United States. | Obesity in women—United States—Psychological aspects. | African American women—Health and hygiene. | African American women—Psychology | Body image in women—United States.
Classification: LCC RC552.O25 C69 2020 | DDC 362.1963/980092 [B]—dc23
LC record available at https://lccn.loc.gov/2020006712

1 2 3 4 5 6 7 8 9 MARQUIS 25 24 23 22 21 20

This book includes recycled material and material from well-managed forests. North Atlantic Books is committed to the protection of our environment. We print on recycled paper whenever possible and partner with printers who strive to use environmentally responsible practices.

Let's try to get together. And strive to be yourself and not somebody else . . . I've seen so many black women throughout this country. Two years ago, they was very white. This evening they are so black that you don't know them. The only thing you have to be that's important in life—to make yourself, your husband or whoever it is very happy—is just go on being your own normal, black beautiful selves as women, as human beings.

—FANNIE LOU HAMER

CONTENTS

FOREWORD

By Ta'lor L. Pinkston, The Heart Advocate

ike most girls, I struggled with body image issues, and guess what? I am a grown ass woman and I still struggle with body image issues. At my smallest and at my biggest, I body shamed myself. If you have ever been considered plus-size, thick, or fat, you can relate to stories of bullying, verbal and physical abuse, and the disrespectful comments from family and friends.

I first noticed the stretch marks on my sides when I was in fifth grade. I was so insecure about them because stretch marks meant I was getting fat. I grew up knowing that I would never be *allowed* to wear a belly shirt (that's what we called crop tops at the time) or a two-piece swimsuit, or put on anything thin girls could wear. At age ten, I was aware that I had to hide my stretch marks and belly rolls because they were not beautiful or a part of the *standard of beauty.*

When I went to college, I was the biggest I have ever been; and after gaining the *freshman fifteen,* spending eight years living college life, and having a beautiful baby girl, my belly was and is now covered in stretch marks. I continued to hide my body from the world because of my fear of judgment and ridicule from family, friends, and society as a whole (especially on social media) because I knew that my natural body was now far from the beauty standard of flawless skin.

Although this is a story many girls can relate to, *Black girls* share a different experience because our story involves an added layer of colorism.

I grew up knowing that a woman who is fair-skinned, size 00–10, five-foot-five to five-foot-seven, with long hair, hazel eyes, full lips, flawless skin, and a curvy body type (full breasts, small waist, and full hips and booty) was considered more attractive. I knew, like most Black girls, that if you do not meet or come close to that standard, you will likely be impacted by the discrimination and hatred that comes with this bias.

Joy Cox has reminded me that I have body and beauty privilege that protected me from the discrimination and disparities of being a fat Black girl. Now at age thirty, I am over 240 pounds, wearing a size 18 in jeans; and although I am more aware of the privilege in my skin tone and my body type, I have never heard the story of what it would be like for me in my relationships, personal life, and professional development if I was bigger and had darker skin growing up.

Most Black people understand that *colorism is a problem* in the POC community. There are many Black people who judge other Black people for their skin tone. My mother and adopted older sister are both dark-skinned, my father is a little lighter than me, and my younger sister and I are about the same skin shade. I learned to love every shade of brown in my household, but outside of my home, the Black community did not always show the same acceptance.

I learned that because I was brown-skinned, I was considered *more attractive* than my sister and my cousins who were darker than me. Even with my type 4 hair, I had beauty privilege because my brown skin was not too dark and I had light brown eyes. It was not until I started gaining weight that I realized how much my privilege and my lack of privilege impacted my childhood.

Since I was introduced to Joy Cox, I have witnessed her clear intention to share how the biases against fat Black bodies impacted her and other fat Black girls. Joy is challenging her readers to do three things:

1. To understand how we fit or do not fit in the standard of beauty

2. To stop avoiding tough topics around fatphobia and colorism

3. To challenge our biases around girls' bodies, fat bodies, Black bodies, and fat Black girls' bodies

Joy's no-nonsense approach to storytelling challenged me to think about how I perpetuate fatphobia and colorism as a Black girl. With every word, I was forced to look at how these social concerns impacted my life, my family and friends, and even my community as a whole. After reading, I feel that I am more capable of being a fat-acceptance abolitionist and acknowledging my own privilege.

Fat Girls in Black Bodies shares the experiences of a Black girl's struggle with discrimination and prejudice in dating and relationships, in the classroom, at church, at family reunions, during holidays, and in the workplace as a professional. The best part about what Joy represents is that she doesn't shy away from calling anyone out: White supremacy, beauty standards, body type privilege in the plus-size community, the lack of representation of darker skin in the LGBTQIA+ community, and even the Black community, who all display fatphobic and colorism biases. It brought me literal *joy* to read such a raw vulnerability and passion for fat Black femme acceptance.

I am honored to have this opportunity to share how Joy has impacted me by sharing her truth. Body shaming is something every girl can relate to, but not every girl has heard what body shaming looks like with a lack of privilege. Representation matters, and Joy Cox is holding space for a cohort in the Black community that are crying out to be seen and to be heard.

There is so much value and need for celebrating fat girls in Black bodies, and I hope that you read and feel that you have a responsibility as an ally/abolitionist or that you feel seen as a fat Black girl.

PREFACE

SOMETIMES, IT BE YOUR OWN FAMILY

There we were. All standing in line waiting to get lifted up by my dad, who was about six-foot-one. I was about five or six years old at the time. My dad would often come to our house and visit. By this point, he and my mom had terminated their romantic relationship, but he was always close enough to take a drive to the projects to see his kids. He always made an entrance with loud music and the cologne you could smell around the corner. This is how I typically knew he was around! I mean, before I ever heard him or saw his face, I could smell him. It energized me so. I was always excited to see him for the most part when I was younger. My sisters and I would all run to greet him, and he would do the "thing." He'd pick us up and put us down. It was such a simple gesture. Looking back, if someone would have told me I'd only grow to be five-foot-four (and a half!), being six feet, if only for a few seconds, would have had so much more meaning.

As we stood in line, my dad lifted my older sister first. Straight up and back down. There were smiles and giggles all the ways through. I was so excited to go next! I'm sure my cheeks were the same size today as they were thirty years ago. I was beaming from ear to ear. As my sister stepped out of the way, I moved forward for my opportunity to see new heights. My dad lifted me high. Straight up and back down. But unlike what he did with my sister, letting her walk away, he said something to me that made me ponder its meaning for years. He gave me a warning. He told me he would not be able to keep picking me up like he had done for so long. During that time, I was more perplexed than anything else. I wondered why. Why would he have to stop? More so, I also questioned why he would have to stop with *only* me? What was it about me that would cause this fun in my life to cease? It couldn't have been my age, because my sister was older. It couldn't have been my height, because I wasn't the tallest.

This was my first recollection of what it meant to belong while not *really* belonging. I was heavier than my older sister and did not live regularly in an environment that made this evident (or relevant, for that matter). For most of my childhood, my family and I lived with my grandmother (who was really my aunt, but that's a story for another day), who also lived with her daughter and grandbaby. It was seven of us in a two-bedroom, two-story house in the projects. My aunt (the grandmother's daughter), Pearl, was a fat, dark-skinned woman who was the epitome of fun. She was my first exposure to what living in a larger body looked like, and BOY was it fabulous! Pearl was one of them cool aunts. We had the baddest sound system in the projects! She knew new music before we did. She dressed to impress, always. Throwing parties should've been her life's work. We weren't even allowed to call her "aunt." Pearl would do just fine. She said she was too young for that. She was Black, fat, and *all-la-dat*! (as my dad would say). And as I too was becoming fat and *all-la-dat,* I got a lot of identity cues from her. We were, simply, normal. We never talked about fat in a negative way. We never discussed fat bodies as something to avoid. Granted, there were times when I saw the SlimFast shakes, but the conversation around the body she had was never framed as a body she needed to rid herself from. So imagine how my five/six-year-old self felt hearing this new language from my father. Imagine my five/six-year-old self attempting to process what he was trying to say. Though I believe that his intent was not to harm me or hurt my feelings (if he were alive, I think he would be surprised to know that I still remember this), this is the FIRST time I can remember something negative being said about my weight. That's some heavy shit. Often those closest to us have the ability to hurt us the most because our guard can be down. In fact, as research states, most daughters get their first impressions of their bodies from their mothers. Fat acknowledgment also has been recorded to take place in toddlers as young as three years old. One would think that most three-year-olds do not have a solid friendship circle at this age. Therefore, those inscribing children with labels of fatness FIRST are more likely to be parents, other family members, and family friends.

Whew! If I would've known back then what I know now, I would've cherished the time my aunt and I spent just being. I would've basked in the environment where fatness did not come with a moral judgment. My aunt had friends and romantic partnerSSSSssss. I'm emphasizing the fact that she had more than one, because men have ALWAYS loved fat women despite what they say. And this is not a statement to validate her value, but rather a statement of fact. At the time, I had no idea my life was getting ready to be caught up in a whirlwind of "different." That "different" would last for a good decade before I would start to see some light at the end of the tunnel. I had a foundation set in body acceptance that would be tried and tested on every hand. I would also lose the closest connection to belonging through relocation. Being in this body, I had to learn how to survive early. Shit, I'm still learning how to survive now! Nevertheless, time waited for no one, and the very warning my father gave me after what would be one of my last lifts was a precursor to the fat hatred that stood at the door of my evolution.

UPROOTED AND SEARCHING

When I was seven, my mom decided to relocate and move me and my sisters to Johnstown, Pennsylvania. This was roughly four and a half hours away from Philadelphia, where I had been born and raised. Philly had been all I'd ever known. I had friends there. My safe haven (my grandmom) was there. I *belonged.* Aside from the stress of going somewhere new, I wasn't made aware that we'd be moving until the day of. I watched my cousins cry before any announcement was made and started crying too. Why? I didn't know. But I figured there had to be a reason. Seeing people sad made me sad. I knew nothing about being an empath. When I realized people were crying because my mother had made the decision to move my sisters and me away from the only family I had ever known, I cried and could not be consoled. Perhaps this is why my mother didn't want to tell me? I felt like I was losing myself. A piece of me arguably died that day.

I remembered crying myself to sleep, waking up, and finishing where I left off. Arriving in Johnstown, I hated it. I hated where we slept. I hated that the food was not the same. I hated that I could not just walk down a flight of stairs and see my family. What does one do for a child with depression at the age of seven? What does a child with depression at the age of seven do? Watching TV shows like *Lamb Chop's* instead of *Duck-Tales* also sucked! We stayed with my uncle and his family until my mom was able to get her own place. That dwelling wasn't home to me. I never felt settled. I was simply existing, waiting for a change that could better my situation. For those who think that kids don't get "it" or understand the changes that happen around them, allow me to be one to say that we do! Maybe I wasn't aware of the implications of moving, but I knew things had changed. I knew I was disconnected from feeling secure. I also knew what heartbreak felt like. I distinctly remember crying to Mariah Carey's "Love Takes Time" when it played and I thought about my grandmother. I also remember making up stories to fit in, because I wasn't sure what I needed to do to become friends with people in a new place. It also didn't help that the year I began school, I was also forced to acknowledge that my size was different.

The year was 1989, and my mom had finally got a place! I don't know how long we were at my uncle's, but those months seemed like a lifetime. By now, my experience of "different" was evolving, and I started to notice things I hadn't before. For example, my dad was sending me and my sister matching outfits . . . in matching sizes. Those "MC Hammer" pants were fresh! I had a turquoise set while my sister had purple. We also had matching jean dress jumpers too. Man, with a fresh dose of Vaseline that greased up our calves, you couldn't tell us NOTHING! We were sisters sharing clothes and looking like twins, albeit my sister was two years older than me. That didn't matter to me though. I thought it was cute. Over time, my harem pants began to look more like tights, and my jumper was hard to pull up over my hips. I had to say goodbye to those before my sister. To replace them with something just as stylish but larger was not an option. At school, I wasn't the only Black child in class, but I was the only fat Black girl. The snickers and chuckles I heard when playing kickball were enough to know that people saw something different in how I ran, played, or existed. And these chuckles weren't the type I was supposed to join in on. No, these were the whispered chuckles. The type that when you look back, others stop laughing. By fifth grade, I started to be more self-conscious of my body. Being weighed in the nurse's office was one of the first times I started to be ashamed of how much I weighed. Notes came home with a list of recommendations for me to slim down. Even as a child, I was pissed about this, because I too had no idea the changes my body was going through. I couldn't explain how I ate what everyone else did and played like everyone else, but yet didn't look the part. I resented the fact that doctors made assumptions about what I ate and did not do. I couldn't explain why I didn't *belong*. I also couldn't understand why everyone was so hell-bent on me belonging according to standards we all knew I wasn't meeting.

By the age of ten, I was shopping in the Misses section of clothing stores. I often dressed ten years my senior. Graduating from the fifth grade, I did so in a cream-colored blazer and lace palazzo pants! Now, in fairness, the pants today would be fire! But at the time, not being able to find clothes in my size for my age was a huge signal that I had no place. Though I was ten, it was pretty clear the kids section of clothing stores had no love for my thighs. It was also becoming more apparent that the Misses section wasn't exactly ready for me either. Pants were too long. Blouses were too . . . blousy. I was a thirty-five-year-old fifth grader. My shorts were grown. My shirts were grown. Shit, my underwear was grown too! Clothing store selections repeatedly screamed at me to find another place to find what I needed. But where is that place? After all, we're talking about needs here. Where could I go to get big girl drawls at the age of ten? My one silver lining in clothing choices was a bathing suit I had acquired from somewhere in order to take swimming lessons. To this day, I still don't know how I was chosen for the program, but in fifth grade I had the privilege of leaving school early to go to the "Y" (MCA) and learn how to swim. I had an all-black bathing suit with white polka dots. It was fabulous! I am forever grateful to my mom for finding it. It was a one-piece swimsuit. I felt acceptable in it. I didn't worry about my body. I didn't worry about my weight. Even those that instructed me didn't seem to be bothered. Escaping school if even for a half-day to get my hair wet and stripped of its moisture for the day was worth it. There was such a freeing presence. It may have been because I was actually free from other kids' chuckles or the demands of school nurses, but why didn't matter. In that place, I *belonged*. I learned how to swim on top of and under water. My brown skin in that polka-dotted bathing suit was all I needed. I backstroked to freedom if only for a few weeks. That suit was my saving grace. I didn't know how much I needed it until I had it.

LABELS, LABELS, LABELS

As the summer of 1992 approached, I did what I always had done as a child. I played with friends and readied myself to make a visit back to Philly. I always loved this time of the year, because it gave me the opportunity to see family and familiarize myself again with the environment I held dear. Every year, my sisters and I would visit my family for the summer. Three months of unadulterated fun! *DuckTales*, soft pretzels, water ice, and Double Dutch. There was a public pool in walking distance, and old friends would know we were coming, so we were never at a loss to find folks to play with. We packed our bags and waited for my dad to make the trip. He would arrive in some fancy car he'd just bought and take us over the mountains. By this point, the relationship I had with my father was, for a lack of better words, awkward. We didn't talk as much, and those lift rides stopped ages ago. There were also other narratives of fatness I was now contending with that I hadn't had to before. Often being the one who was seen as mature or outspoken, I had this label of adult-likeness I had to deal with. Now, for my older sister, she had a label of defiance. Everyone seen her as the rebel. My younger sister was the baby. But for me, this mammy-like, feisty, mama-wannabe narrative was being crafted of me, and in many ways simply did not fit. I did not want to be the person who always spoke up, but when a question was asked and your sisters remained silent, I guess I was the only one who spoke up.

Additionally, I never wanted to be seen as older or more mature. As I would later learn, these labels are often given to fat Black girls. Moreover, little Black girls are often seen as older and more "adult-like" than their White counterparts. A report from 2017 by researchers at Georgetown Law's Center on Poverty and Inequality found that in a survey of 325 participants, Black girls are seen as needing less nurturing, support, and comfort (Epstein, Blake, and González 2017). They're also considered to be more independent and knowledgeable about adult topics, which include sex. As a result, their childhoods are often stripped from them through the process of "othering." They are separated and treated as culpable for behaviors through "adultification" bias. Through this lens, there is no mercy given to them like that given to White children or other children of color. No room is left for understanding. They are guilty as charged for behaviors that are interpreted through a slanted perspective of the Black experience, another consequence of White supremacy. Subsequently, based on a follow-up study with focus groups, Georgetown continued their Girlhood Interrupted project along with starting the hashtag #letblackgirlsbegirls. The findings can be located on Georgetown Law's website. This time around, the focus groups were conducted with young Black girls reading the responses of those from the first study to gauge their reactions. Time and time again, young Black girls recounted stories about how they were treated harsher for the same behaviors as their classmates who were not Black. It should be a crime to be held to a standard of perfection in order to contend with the mediocrity that is lauded and practiced routinely by White folks.

Looking back, this all makes perfect sense, but at the time, I had no idea why people would not just let me be a kid. I mean, sure, I was still a kid, but I wasn't the cute little girl growing up to be a woman. No, I skipped all that and was on the cusp of being catapulted right into puberty! I was pissed! I didn't want to be the person who was considered the most responsible or smartest or the "old soul"! Over time, I grew into those roles, but damn, it would've been nice to just sit and play Nintendo most days unbothered. Even to this day, my older sister makes it a point to tell people she's the oldest. Growing up, I never saw why.

I wasn't so cute like my sisters (even in one's defiance). I also didn't look so cute in my outfits like them. Most of my clothes were used as a tool to cover me more than dress me. Oversized T-shirts with shorts down to my knees were often my #ootd. I can only imagine what my mother felt like having to find something for me to wear at my age. Probably a lot like how I felt until more recently trying to find something my age in the Plus sections. No fun, bright colors. No cartoons. Nothing that made me feel good about having a belly or chunky thighs. No space for me to be fat and belong.

By the summer of 1992, chatter had begun among family members. There were all types of talk about what I was eating and what I was not. People wondered if I was playing Nintendo (I was a *Super Mario* pro!) too much. They wondered what I was eating while my mother wasn't home. They needed to solve my fatness like a mathematical equation. I needed peace. Being back in Philly during the summer was refreshing with acceptance even if it came with a few raised eyebrows. Everyone around me had smaller bodies. I couldn't explain it. Quite frankly, neither could they. The older I got, the more people went out of their way to make the difference known: "Girl, look at your thighs!" "What have you been eating?" And the subtle suggestions for me to be more active, because the assumption was that my body was larger because I hadn't been. I would later learn that the type of body I was developing in had a long history of being rejected and had nothing to do with me personally. I would find that fat-phobia and racism were somehow melded together to make the narrative of the mammy seem like an inheritance more than by design. Running in a race you didn't know you were in is where I stood.

* * *

Looking back over some of these stories, I got choked up because revisiting your survival also means revisiting the pain. Being a Black fat child was no "cake walk" (pun intended). I almost wish it was a walk with cake, because that just sounds waaaay better than what I had to endure. At this point in my life, I was still searching for acceptance, security, and safety. I felt different before I was ever aware of being different. It took me quite some time to figure out that you cannot undo some things in life, but you can learn how to process them differently. Being made aware of my fat forever changed how I saw myself and the world around me. It showed me that the world is not always safe, and even those who mean best can hurt you. I knew I could not survive simply relying on others. I understood I had to be my own advocate. I had no idea I'd find community. I had no idea I'd find myself.

Part 1

Black People,
Black Culture,
Black Fat

1

WHERE IT ALL BEGAN

What can I say about the sect of the Black community I grew up around? At the tender age of thirty-six, I often reflect on the impact being Black has had on my life. Being an '80s baby, I've lived through the transition of VHS to DVD. I was alive during a time when it was not common to have a microwave. Obviously, the internet would come later, but I was here for that transition too. I grew up poor and started my tenure in housing through the projects. Living in the projects was a beautiful thing for me as a kid. My friends lived just a short distance away. There was also a very real feel of community. This is where I first learned the concept of "if I got it, you got it."

I had cousins that weren't. BBQs were community events. No one on our block went without eating. If we didn't have meals, we at least had the ingredients to share so someone could make them. I grew up in a matriarchal household. My gram (who was really my grandaunt) was a G! Gram had stepped in as "Mom" to fill the role with my mother and her siblings after her sister passed away unexpectedly. I looked up to her for her strength and ability to handle business. There was no such thing as gender roles in our house. The rules of who got to do what based on age were also a bit flexible (I believe I was going to the corner store to play numbers by the time I was nine). We learned what we needed to do in order to survive. Everybody had a part to play. Everyone mattered.

My gram at one point was also fat (smaller fat). Her daughter, my aunt, had been fat (mid- to superfat) as long as I could remember. Then there was me. Under one roof, three generations of fat people resided. I had someone to look up to, and these people would also understand my needs. I had a vision before me that showcased what success looked like in a body like mine. My aunt was so vibrant! She partied and loved life in a way that it oozed out her pores. Everyone wanted to get to Pearl's parties! She danced. She sang. She had a smile that would light up a room. Pearl was a dark-skinned, fat Black woman. Her skin was smooth. The kind of smooth available via filters on these picture apps. She knew the latest songs. She recorded episodes of *Friday Night Videos* so we could too. She was the epitome of fun. I wanted to be like that.

My gram was the enforcer. She was the person you came to if somebody crossed you. She'd be the person counting money in the back while the guests enjoyed themselves. She was also the only one that could manage to get the family together for occasions. Gram had this black telephone book that was almost impossible to navigate if you didn't know where to look. I'm not even sure it had the letter tabs so you could find the person by name. She would just tell us to go get her book, and magically, people would appear at the next shindig. She was stern but caring. I think her propensity to keep the family together illustrated that. No doubt, she also liked to party. I think my whole family did, honestly. The way I saw it, if I could learn how to balance the personalities of my gram and my aunt, I'd be the perfect person.

The size of my belly or hips simply did not matter in this version of the world they had crafted. What mattered was if you could do the choreography to the latest Janet Jackson video (I could). What mattered was if you were having a good time (I was). I also lived with my mother, two sisters, and cousin. They were slender in size. I thought body diversity was the norm . . . everywhere.

The memory of my gram announcing she had diabetes is one of the most vivid memories I have from my childhood. I remember her being in the kitchen, standing up and reporting back what the doctors had said. I also remember her being very nonchalant about the diagnosis. She still intended to party, not worried about what the doctors had to say. Despite her sister losing her battle in part to the disease in 1985, she still intended to live her best life. For reference, my gram was slightly over 150 pounds at the time. I know because she used to weigh herself and say the numbers. She had a belly and thicker thighs. Not your stereotypical image of a person diagnosed with type 2 diabetes, although statistics will show that people assigned to the "normal or slightly overweight" group actually do lead the numbers in diagnoses (LeWine 2012). We'd go on to be graced by her presence for another ten years. She took her last breath in August of 2000.

Losing Gram was like losing a piece of myself. I remember losing it in the bathroom of the Amtrak station as I waited to catch a train back to culinary arts school in Pittsburgh. There wasn't enough tissue in the bathroom for all the tears and snot that ran out of my face. I had just lost one of the most important factors in my life! I gave no fucks about cooking! I could care less about grades and the daily mundane bullshit of academics! I wanted my gram back! I wanted to talk to her again over the phone and see her face. I wanted to rub my hand through her ultra-soft hair and look into her dark brown eyes. This was some bullshit! I rode back on that Amtrak train with bloodshot eyes and a hole in my heart. I had never felt such loss in my life. My family didn't believe in funerals, and my gram was adamant about being cremated. There was no official "goodbye" besides the one I created for myself to honor her memory. For weeks I called my mom and, intuitively knowing, she'd tell me stories about my gram until I was ready to go to bed. It eased my mind and warmed my heart. I feared forgetting what her voice sounded like. I hated losing her! Over time, the phone calls to my mom became less frequent. I could remember Gram and smile. Moreover, what I'd come to realize was that the memories she'd leave with me had such a value. I'd remember them when I felt like I wasn't being treated like I mattered. I'd remember them when I needed to think of ways I could treat myself and feel better. When I was three years old, Gram used to sneak me out of the house in the mornings to go eat breakfast at the diners. She dubbed me her "most favorite one of all"! She was an escape for me. A safe place in childhood where I could take refuge. The foundation set for me as a fat Black kid started out well, but would get rocky along the way.

I know it is typically thought that Black folk accept fat. And shit, maybe some do. In the landscapes of southern Nigeria, they do. In many Arab nations, they do (BBC News 2007). In the whispers away from what's trending on TV and in magazines, they do. HOWEVER. What I will say, in my case, and the case of some of my comrades involved in this work: this simply has not been the case. There have been many ups and downs of the accept/reject tension in the Black community as it relates to body size and fat. There is no black-and-white area of acceptance. Just as I watched my aunt have many friends and lovers in her pocket of the universe, I also watched fat Black friends get ghosted, made fun of, and played by members of our community. Factors that play heavily into whether fat bodies are accepted in the community revolve around not just how big your body may be, but also what shape and complexion that body comes in (*Go Off Sis!* 2019). Proximity to White, European beauty aesthetics also determines one's ability to assimilate into what could be deemed the general consensus of acceptance in the Black community (Patton 2006). I don't know if it needs to be said, but I stand to remind folk that the natural hair craze is still rather new. Black women—especially Black fat women—were not exactly praised by their community for embracing their locs or tightly coiled strands until recently. Rather "exotic" looks of Blackness were valued more so than your everyday "round the way" girl.

The added pressure of being fat in all the "right" places also does not help. And I don't care how many slimming contraptions (here's looking at you, waist trimmers) you buy, research is clear that in the event one loses weight, one does not get to determine where it comes off at (Gwinup, Chelvam, and Steinberg 1971). Collectively, we can say in unison, the idea of having an ultra-slim waist and fat ass is un-fucking-realistic. The ability to harness large amounts of fat in one's breasts, butt, and hips on tiny frames only aids in the objectification of bodies for the patriarchal gaze. Indeed, diet culture exists in the Black community, even if it presents itself in a different form.

Thick thighs (that is, thighs that have a decent amount of fat on them without the appearance of cellulite, or thighs that meticulously balance the fat-to-muscle ratio without thigh fat spilling over in an unfavorable way) are desired. You need to have enough fat to jiggle when you walk but not so much that you jiggle when you do everything else. After all, "real" women have cleavage. "Real" women should also be able to double as a man's pillow at will if need be. Raised under this patriarchal vomit, the idea is that this man, whoever he is, should be able to find comfort in a woman's body, and a "healthy" (read as sizable) amount of fat helps to accomplish this. However, things get sketchy when your fat compounds. Dimples fill your thighs, the fat around your triceps begins to hang, and your belly develops a "pouch." Your face develops extra "chins" (it never actually develops more than one but, whatever), your butt spreads in width but doesn't protrude outward, and the cleavage of your breasts doesn't quite measure up in fullness. Your shape resembles more of a circle than a pear or Coke bottle.

In this space, the blame begins. People wonder what you could've done (or not) to wind up the way you are. How can you be so big with none of the features that make a Black body beautiful? How could you be so big with the features that make a Black body beautiful and let them go to waste by being so big? This is the so big that people smile in your face but laugh at jokes about your body type in private. The so big that romantic prospects second-guess claiming you in public.

It wasn't long before I began to realize these truths in my own life. Around family, there was sort of this sense of protection but also threat from those who did not know how to keep their mouths shut. I found myself being quickly ushered into fat friend roles that I didn't even know existed. There was the motherly fat friend, the undateable fat friend that was cool with the guys, the strong-arm fat friend that would be feisty when necessary, the friendly fat friend that was too nice and sacrificed a lot in exchange for validation from the "in" crowd, and the clown. All these roles being influenced by both my size and race. In some of these roles, I saw my aunt and my gram, so I took to them naturally. Yet, the feeling was different. I did not feel empowered, I felt exploited. I felt used and abused by folks who said they liked me. They were some damn liars! The tables of friendship were often lopsided, with me giving more than I would ever get in exchange. The heart-crushing disappointment of knowing the same people who befriended you also made jokes about your size behind your back was enough to make anyone vow to *never* trust someone to defend your body in its absence.

Building up a defense to fend off the bullshit was *always* in the back of my mind. While I did understand that I wasn't in the running for the next People's Choice Award, I wasn't going to allow folks to treat me any old kind of way, believing that I was insignificant. Did I really need acceptance that bad? The answer for me was an astounding "Hell nah!" Armed with a CD player, fresh batteries, and loud enough earphones to tune out voices, my tranquility rested in music. I didn't need friends! Of course I did. To be clear, I didn't need two-faced friends like the ones I was seeming to attract. Being alone was safer. I was a happy loner. I learned to find my strengths and build a character that would ensure I'd never treat people how people who claimed to be my friends treated me. The consequence to this was that I was also becoming skillful in shutting people out. There was a time when I prided myself on the emotional wall I built that no one would be able to scale. I started building my fortress for protection. Shutting people out and cutting them off were both weapons I slept close to at night.

The cost of weight stigma is enormous for those who encounter it. The loss of interpersonal interaction limits access that fat individuals have to building friendships, romantic relationships, and networks for upward mobility (Emmer, Bosnjak, and Mata 2020). Emotionally, weight stigma takes its toll on recipients by eroding trust and compounding stress and anxiety. As a result, the impacts of weight stigma become negative outcomes manifested in the lives of fat people worldwide (Dolezal and Lyons 2017). They do not create meaningful relationships. They stay indoors to avoid people and "othering." They suffer when it comes to employment and networking. People in larger bodies earn less than those who are smaller. They are also perceived as less apt to do the jobs they were hired to do. There have been instances where prospective employees were denied clearance by health professionals due to weight stigma. Additionally, current employees have expressed less confidence in a larger co-worker's ability to complete their job, limiting collaboration efforts and upward mobility. Adding what it means to be Black and womxn to this context, there is added oppression intersecting across identities, making it extremely hard to get out from under. The advice given to those *even* in the Black community? Lose weight.

In understanding the struggle of fat Black girls, it is short-sighted not to include my sisters in the LGBTQ+ community. I see y'all! Our experiences are different, although they converge at times. The recklessness of cishetero norms forced onto the bodies and narratives of nonbinary and genderqueer folx actually puts some in danger of losing their lives. The majority of transgender murders in 2019 were of Black womxn (Kaur 2019). The struggle for pronouns to be acknowledged is *still* ongoing in the United States, despite the *Merriam-Webster Dictionary* appointing the pronoun "they" as the 2019 word of the year (Merriam-Webster 2019).

So what is it like to be fat, Black, and queer in the Black community? As someone who is cisgender, I do not want to take up space attempting to explain this, because I cannot. However, I do want to shed light on the topic, as I feel this is something that needs to be discussed. I prefer to use those in the communities I have come across as a "voice," understanding we only become better by providing space, not hoarding it for ourselves. The constant tension to balance identities while managing the truth held within oneself can leave those in the community feeling lost and without support. Cicely Blain sums up her experience perfectly, stating, "I was too big to be a child, too masculine to be a girl, too black to be innocent and too fat to be pretty" (Blain 2019, 11).

Even within the Black community, there can be disdain for those who do not fit into the norms of mainstream society. With each additional marker of difference, the struggle intensifies. The comments of misinformation and ignorance about gender and

sexual identities grow (Rose 2018). Feelings are hurt, with healing never being administered. To be fat, Black, and queer is to
also be seen as subhuman, deserving of hurt and pain (Battle and
Ashley 2008).

The LGBTQ+ community does not have the same affordances
to "skate" through Black society unnoticed. A body that cannot
be hidden coupled with an identity not always readily seen creates a sense of being both hypervisible and invisible. There is
indeed extra labor taken up in playing the part of a cisgender
individual, particularly if you are expected to present as the ste-
reotyped feminine woman. The extra lengths taken to do femme
things, talk femme ways, and participate in culture that has no
space to respect your individuality can easily leave some folx at
their wit's end. To add, activists like Ilya of Decolonizing Fitness
speak to the difficulties within the trans community, where body
dysmorphia is common and stems from societal norms (Dockray
2017). The constant push-and-pull tension of seeing a body that
doesn't reflect the gender you identify with, along with the pressure of what communities *say* certain bodies should look like, is
daunting, confusing, and downright tormenting. Nevertheless,
the Black community is not exempt from placing these demands
on its members.

According to the Williams Institute in 2012, roughly 40 percent of homeless youth are also part of LGBT communities,
with 43 percent of them being forced out of their homes due to
rejection of their sexual identities by their parents, and 46 percent running away for the same reason (Durso and Gates 2012).
The ills of homophobia do not shorten their hands in the Black
community. The compounded impact of fatphobia simply makes
them heavier.

Reports of the difference in treatment extend far beyond
the Black community, as fat Black queer femmes have faced
scrutiny in education and health care settings. Walela Nehanda

spoke with Taylor Crumpton to document their experience with the barriers to quality health care after their diagnosis of blood cancer (Crumpton 2019). They were constantly met with dismissal of and disregard for symptoms that clearly signaled something was wrong. Stereotypical assumptions about being a drug addict were present when they visited emergency rooms. Allyship in this space was scarce. Only one nurse advocated that they be tested for cancer, which eventually led to the proper diagnosis. Walela, an overcomer of eating disorders, also had to contend with European beauty standards as they grappled with treatment. What does a fat Black body going through cancer look like? What *should* it look like? In the end, Walela took an approach to holistic health that allowed them to access needed care that aided in their recovery while maintaining their dignity.

I wish I could say that experiences like Walela's are uncommon. Personally, I have experienced similar treatment as a fat Black woman in health centers. In 2016, I had to switch gynecologists after my former one attempted to slide me that nonsensical weight loss sheet upon my checkout. Y'all know the sheet! The one that swears you only need to make small changes like cutting 500 calories from each meal to achieve weight loss and live a more blissful life. They tend to leave out how that bliss turns into anguish though, when your weight boomerangs back in two years or less and you sit in self-pity with disordered eating patterns believing it was your fault. I was later told by my gyno that "we both know" that the reason I had experienced a pulmonary embolism and DVT the year prior was because of my weight, although my own health chart specified it was due to birth control medicine I had been taking. Yeah, fuck that guy! My fingers could not type fast enough that health professionals like him are part of the problem in health care with fat patients. I don't think he ever let his staff know we "broke up." I still get annual pap smear reminders from them to this day.

In 1999, it took three trips and a very angry mother before doctors would do an X-ray of my chest and abdomen to see what was wrong with me. Three instances of getting up at all hours of the night with horrid abdominal pain to be rushed to the emergency room via taxi (we didn't have a car), only to be told that nothing was wrong. Turns out, something *was* wrong, and I was kept in the hospital for a week, being prepped for gallbladder surgery. I was sixteen. Imagine if my mother was not there to advocate for me? How worse would my condition have gotten? And to think, once the problem was identified, I was told by the physician, the one who would do the procedure, to stop eating so much fried chicken! I wanted to throat punch him! I wanted to scream at the top of my lungs that it wasn't the chicken! I didn't know the term fatphobia at the time, but I was very familiar with being treated differently because of my size by health professionals. That night, I had to choose between getting treatment or going to jail. My stomach hurt too much to throat punch that man. Instead, I resorted to telling my family, who chuckled and really didn't get why I was offended. I wanted to throat punch them too! Such blatant language wrapped in fatphobia and racism should never be okay.

When the film *Precious* came out, I could relate. People who are "thick" could not. Precious was considered unattractive, unfriendly, uneducated, and absolutely unlovable (in the platonic or romantic sense). She was a castaway by her family and society at large. Her dark complexion and large belly did not bode well even for friendship. Sapphire wrote the book *Push* that the film is based on because this was a reality she had encountered multiple times in her line of work as a remedial reading teacher in Harlem, New York (NPR 2009). What is to be said about the ways that the Black community finds those who are dark-skinned, fat, and read as unattractive to be disposable among us? Would we be possibly discussing a different outcome if Precious was educated and fat with a pear or Coke bottle figure? Damn right. I perceive that the Black community indeed has a blind spot in our view as we lament about our treatment by others. And this is not to say that what we lament about is not warranted. It is also not to say that we should lower our voices about what we are lamenting about. Rather, it is a pause for introspection. It's a moment to investigate the infiltration of individualistic-driven standards and how they spoil the most vulnerable among us. All too often when those in the community face more discrimination and hurt at our hands, the first thing yelled is that they, we, are causing division. That's bullshit! They, we, are stating facts. Facts that need to be addressed if we *all* are going to get a place of liberation. It costs the comedian nothing to stop telling fat, homophobic, and transphobic jokes. Nothing! If they couldn't get someone to laugh outside of these contexts, they should consider a new profession. To add, what is the cost to families, friends, or lovers to acknowledge our presence? Social capital is a helluva drug! Indeed, that which is individualistic will at some point converge with others to become a collective. Otherwise, how is it possible that Precious could have received the same type of rejection from several different individuals at different points in her life? How is it that so many can relate to her story while still seeking shelter from the individuals who reside in their homes, schools, jobs, and elsewhere? Where has our courage gone to hashtag #blacklove when it comes to all of us and not just the arrangements that are aesthetically pleasing to the dominant voices in the community?

I'd be lying if I said I never thought that the weight of my gram or my aunt contributed to their health complications. From as long as I can remember, fatness and diseases like diabetes have gone hand in hand. Many members in the Black community think because you are fat, getting diabetes is just a matter of time. They tell stories about your uncles, aunts, and cousins who suffered this fate, having to become amputees because of "suga." If you are a midsize (think size 22–24) to superfat (size 26–32), you by all accounts are the type of fat that no one wants to be. You are Precious. Unfriendly, not worthy of being heard, and absolutely headed for heart disease. Perhaps the idea that fat accompanies sickness was a reason for their concern and disgust? It's hard to say. We are often told in our community that we are more likely to suffer from strokes, diabetes, and hypertension without a full explanation as to why (Mays, Cochran, and Barnes 2007; Turner, n.d.; Abdullah et al. 2017). Food is seen as the precursor to our illnesses (Norton 2018), and though we deviate little from how we feed one another, the person who possesses the body is ultimately blamed for how their body turns out.

The Black community is inundated by a diet culture stemming from White supremacy but repurposed based on our own aesthetics. For example, the celebration around bodies that are shaped favorably is the result of the same food used to shame those whose bodies are not considered desirable. If cousin Trina has a sizable ass and smaller waist, this is because of the cornbread and greens she consumes. If cousin Rochelle has a large waist with a large flat ass, this is because of the cornbread and greens she consumes. To quote the former member of the Black delegation for common sense that was Kanye West, "How Sway?!?" Stretch marks to denote growth of favorable body parts are acknowledged as a good thing regardless of age (i.e., to be younger and have stretch marks on your hips or butt was acceptable because it just meant your body was growing in the "right" way; to have stretch marks on your knees meant you would grow and be tall); however, stretch marks in any other area give pause and concern. I remember the agony and disappointment I felt at the age of twelve when I noticed stretch marks had made their way to my belly. I remember being saddened and feeling like a failure because at least from my understanding as an adolescent, people who have not been pregnant should not have stretch marks on their belly. I remember daydreaming of the days when I would *actually* be pregnant, to mask the "damage" I had done to my own body. The irreversible damage that could not be covered by makeup or Palmer's stretch mark cream. There wasn't enough cocoa butter in the world that could massage the rippled, dark, uneven lines that ran perpendicular to my belly button. I could not wash them away. I could not even explain why they had appeared when they did. In the end, I had one full, shiny, well-moisturized belly that I vowed to not show until after I had babies, because then my scars would make sense. As long as I vowed to hide these, I knew I would be safe from criticism. No one would have to see them. I'm pretty sure my mother didn't see my belly until after I had gallbladder surgery at the age of sixteen. Hiding was the norm. It was easier for me and my family. Exposure would mean I'd have to give an explanation. One I did not have. Neither did my family. Within our community, it is a constant push and pull of acceptance not governed by the individual, but it is the individual who will undoubtedly "pay" the cost of how things turn out.

If I had a nickel for every time I heard the phrase "All your body is showing," I'd at least be a hundred thousandnaire by now! I came to learn that this phrase often peddled by Black elders really was an exaggeration in their saying that my knees were out or that my shirt was sleeveless. This phrase, this gaslighting of sorts, often led to fat girls constantly tugging at and adjusting their clothing when there is nothing to be fixed (Butler 2018). The fear that something like an arm or knee is showing that shouldn't be is a peak illustration of fatphobia (Kaye 2019). The message sent is that whatever we have is too much to be shared with others. In fact, it is so much, it is offensive. Why do we want *all* of our body out?! What is it about a fat knee that someone cannot bear to see it? To add here, there is also this notion that fat people are not allowed to be comfortable. We *should* wear cardigans in the summer. We *should* exchange those shorts for long, drapey, can't-see-our-figure-if-you-tried skirts. There is never an acceptable time when *all* of our bodies should be out. Our discomfort in exchange for members' appeasement is a fair transaction. We are silenced once again.

The idea that you could lead a successful life and be found to be attractive is also a doozy. The looks of surprise and disgust on family members' faces when one of us shows up pregnant are enough to write a book. Who. Would. Ever. Willingly. Procreate. With. Someone. Who. Looks. Like. You? Funny, because the flipside to this notion is that we, fat Black girls, are also "fast." We want sexual attention (West 2008). Having more fat on our bodies in certain places, like our thighs, butt, and breasts, often means we attract unwanted sexual attention from individuals. But never mind that; the word on the street is that we are practically desperate for it. What were the odds that we could attract someone who had things going for their lives? What were the odds that we could attract someone that others found attractive? Where was the accountability for people who saw us sexually before we had the hormonal uptick to even know what sexual arousal or attraction was?

Being in this space of rejection from our own community also made us extremely vulnerable to the ploys of those who meant us no good. As victims of sexual assault, no one would believe us (Zidenberg et al. 2019). I mean, who would have the strength to pry our big thighs open against our wanting? When we reported advances being made by older members in our community, who would believe that out of ALLLLLL the people in the neighborhood, they would choose us? Bring an attractive partner home? There has to be an ulterior motive. Bring an attractive partner home and watch other people in your neighborhood shoot their shot because they just *know* that individual is only settling with you and hasn't met them yet.

Growing up Black and fat was not for the faint at heart. Memories flood my mind of a family member being overly concerned about me shoveling snow, believing my heart would burst if I exerted myself too much. I recall another referring to my legs as "tree trunks," a reference I still battle with today. I was eleven. Sly remarks and microaggressions were a common occurrence to what it meant to be fat in my community. No one was mistaking me for being "thick." My thighs had long passed the point of being able to restrict the fat spillage to my inner and outer hips. My belly pouch was visible and full.

There was no end to the concern about my clothes being too tight, my skirt being too high, or my body being too round. And I bought into it. It wasn't long before I saw my legs as tree trunks. Wasn't long before skirts looked so much higher and revealing. To say I struggled with acceptance in my community would be an understatement. I sought small and large changes to comply with the demands of diet culture. Internalizing the stigma is actually not uncommon among marginalized populations (Williams and Annandale 2019). I contemplated letting my Toni Braxton-esque hair grow out to hide my face. Fat women with short hair and fat faces were a "no-no." I tried leggings Spanx, panty (cut off your blood circulation) Spanx, and even packaging tape to "smooth" curves and hide the fat that I had. I'll never forget the sound of the tape as I removed it from my waist after the day of taking family photographs. I'll never forget the smell of the plastic or the feeling of getting away with something. Nobody knew. And I suppose, that's how the Spanx phenomenon is supposed to work, no? I had successfully used packaging tape to possess a figure that everyone was supposed to see as normal or at least not question whether it could be actual. Mission accomplished.

I learned the art of war in fighting weight stigma right in my backyard. Sadly, my family and community members were the first enemies of my body. There may have been an instance or two when my family stood up for me, but overall, I knew if I was to survive this fight I was thrown in, I'd have to do most of the heavy lifting myself. Over time, I shaped my defenses to be skillful and strategic. I learned how to discern looks about my body and shut them down before *anyone* fixed their lips to say a word. I started to understand the infiltration of White supremacy in this space. The pressure to conform to European standards of beauty far outweighs the discussions on weight and health (Patton 2006). Much of what is peddled in the Black community about diabetes, high blood pressure, and incidences of stroke focuses much more on assimilation than remedy (Melton 2018). It is about eating what *they* say and doing activities that *they* approve to have a body that meets *their* guidelines. For example, I was always told that eating salad was the best way to health and weight loss. It wasn't until I was well into my twenties that I realized I did not like lettuce. When I was ready to start cooking again out of the love I had for the craft, I began to realize there are so many other vegetables that can provide the same, if not better, nutrients. I realized I didn't have to pigeonhole my food choices for the sake of doing it the "right" way. I didn't have to make my palate conform to European standards. To add, dancing has always been a staple in the Black community and in my family. It is so common to break out into dance sessions that get your body moving. We dance when we clean, cook, mourn, and celebrate. We're *always* moving if there's a beat. I did not need Jane Fonda's help. I did not need to do whatever the guidelines were of that stupid national fitness standard test in school. I just needed to be myself. My body knew what was good for me.

The fear and shame of living in a fat body come dressed in the same racist, fatphobic bullshit the West has been selling for centuries. And we eat it up (pun intended). We eat it for breakfast, lunch, dinner, and snacks. We look past the confounding variables seen to impact our bodies and lived experiences. We cast off our heritage and legacy of full-bodied dynasties for the sake of acceptance on this side of the world that will never fully accept our bodies as equal (Love 2018). Even as Lizzo has used her platform to call out the industry, looking fabulous in her leotards, her twerking and flute playing will fall on deaf ears and blind eyes when we start talking about what should be considered *real* beauty.

White supremacy is a double-edged sword, cutting as it enters and departs. White supremacy has cut the psyches of White folk, having them believe that their mediocrity is supreme, while chipping away the excellence of Black folk to have us believe that our best will never be good enough. White bodies have become the standard, leaving Black bodies to fight for the scraps of validation within our own communities, when we could easily define a new standard. For Black communities who buy into diet culture, we fat Black folk realize we have no dwelling place even among those who look like us. In our communities, we seek refuge constantly, but often never find it. Where is one to go when there is no clear sign of safety? Who will deliver us from the incessant critique of our family and peers? Perhaps Black Jesus.

ON GROWING UP BEING BLACK AND FAT

Earlier in the chapter I spoke about my own journey in coming into the knowledge that my body was problematic. Turns out, I have not been alone in this experience. Many of the guests on my podcast, *Fresh Out the Cocoon,* had a similar journey.

Body relationship coach Ivy Felicia spoke extensively about her journey in the Black community growing up Black and fat and the impact it had on why she now practices "body peace."

For her, we all may not be in a place where we can love our bodies, but we can be in a place to make peace with them. Ivy began, "In the early years, I was very okay with myself. I was comfortable. . . . I was okay because I didn't see anything wrong with it [my body or size], but it wasn't until I got into adolescence and the teenage years when children started making comments. Sometimes, teachers would make comments. That diet mentality came really early. Teachers would say, 'You need to add a little value' or 'work a little harder.' . . . I started realizing that, wait, okay, there's something wrong. None of us are born with that [knowing] that something is wrong until someone starts to tell us that."

Chè Monique of the Society of Fat Mermaids added to this conversation, also detailing her journey and her relationship specifically with her mother: "I have no recollection of not being fat. My dad used to call me 'Bruiser' as a toddler. By the time I was nine, and she [my mom] was pregnant with my youngest brother, I weighed more than her and knew that. As an adult, I'm like, I should have never known that. But you get a lot of flack when you're a child, your mother's pregnant, and you weigh more than her. . . . My mother is the most important person I know, but in terms of my relationship to my weight, we got off with the wrong start."

Lastly, Jai Mobley, owner of Fat Mermaids, talked about her journey in using fashion through her "IDGAF About Your Diet Susan" shirt as an outlet to change the indoctrination around fat bodies and herself: "I want everybody in the world to have this shirt. If you don't have the shirt, I want everybody to feel this. We don't have to deal with people selling us the notion that our bodies are bad, no matter what our bodies look like. I spent a lot of my life feeling bad about the skin I'm in . . . because somebody told me my body was wrong. Basically, that's what it boils down to, because if no one told me something was wrong with me, I wouldn't feel that way."

From these excerpts, it is clear that most of what we learn about our bodies in relation to others happens at a very young age. Having parents, friends, and loved ones take a body-neutral approach by not making moral judgments about our bodies is crucial! And while we can be grateful for who we now have in our community as a result, the question lingers as to what power-houses they'd be if they had not had to have encountered this type of treatment in the first place.

2

GOD AND "HIS" PROBLEM
WITH FAT FOLKS

f you are part of the Black community, chances are you will
find yourself at some point in a church. It could be Baptist,
Pentecostal, or nondenominational. Regardless of the sect, it
will undoubtedly be filled with all the embellishments of Black
culture. You will see it in Sunday attire. You will hear it in the
songs sang. Scripture will be talked about through the eyes of
the culture. There will always be a mother of the church with
stale candy to give to the kids. Religion has been woven into the
fabric of our lives, and we do our best to carry on the legacy of
such from generation to generation.

For many years, I found a space of escape in church. In this
space, I focused a lot less on living up to the expectations of society or the "world" (church folk know what I'm saying), and more
on how I was growing as a person internally. I learned to tuck
and hide my body here the most. Spanx, layers, slips, long skirts,
long shirts, and opaque tights before they were back in style all
adorned my body consistently. In honesty, I no longer knew the

actual silhouette of my body. Other people had to comment to make me aware. I wondered how they knew. It seemed like the more involved in ministry I was, the more I watched myself transform into a caricature of a woman . . . a fat woman. This woman had no need for sexuality and no need to fully embrace her femininity. While others often received guidance and prophecy on marriage and relationships, this fat woman was to focus on studying the Word and serving. While others were provided liberty to embrace living through learning, this fat woman was fashioned to nurture despite having not lived through much at all.

It's easy to get lost and lose yourself in a space as such. It's easy to become the mother, the mature and responsible one, when responsibility is all that you been given. What's it like to be conditioned to be a religious mammy in the name of God? Moreover, what's it like to be that religious mammy and the topic of fat bodies become the subject of sermons delivered on Sunday mornings?

The preacher stood at the pulpit with sweat lightly glistening off his forehead. Towel in hand, he leaned into the mic to speak: "Turn your Bibles to first Corinthians, chapter 15, verse 33. When you get there, say amen." As we turned through the pages, sounds of those who already reached the Scripture began. Grunts, sounds of excitement, and comments like "Come on, Preacher!" in anticipation of the message filled the sanctuary. As I reached the page and said amen, I watched as the preacher took a step back to wipe his brow. When enough of us reached the scriptural destination, he read aloud with emphasis on the words he believed we should take away from the passage. For those who have ever been to or belonged as a member of your typical Black church, you know how this sounds. You also know what it's like to have a preacher stand before you in the pulpit sweating without having done much.

At one point, church was an integral part of my life. I was in that building six days a week at times. More likely the first to arrive and the last to leave. Back then I never really questioned why preachers sweat so much for no reason either. Nevertheless, there I was sitting in the sanctuary preparing myself to hear a few passages on how I could be a better person in Christ. "In Christ" means for a Christian to believe that God's Word (the Bible) is infallible and that it should be followed based on what is written AND interpreted by His (God's) appointed leaders. I prepared my heart to walk away encouraged, ready to tackle my week with a word from the Lord. Whew! I was just as ready as the voices who shouted "Come on, Preacher!" before he went anywhere. I believed this message was just for me.

He shouted "Be not *DECEIVED!*" with the perfect pitch of hominy that only Black preachers can. ". . . evil communications *CORRUPT* good . . . manners." He continued, "I know it may not *SEEEEEM* like the folks you hanging around is looking bad on you, but the *BIIIIIIIIIBLE* is *sayyyyyying,* YOU. ARE. BEING. *CORRUPTED!* And that's not all! It *AIN'T* just about what's being *said, BUT* it's also about what's being *DONE!*" By this point, the church had erupted. Some folks were praising God, while others hung their heads low in shame. By panning the room, it was easy to tell who believed they had allowed themselves to be in the company of those toting "evil" communications. If there'd be an altar call (which there always was), I knew who needed to be there. I also knew that in the event those individuals didn't get to the altar, there'd be some space to chat about their "evil communications" after the service. In the Black church, folks don't believe in going home right after service for some reason. We just hang around and chat, laugh, and do all the things we'd probably be able to do in our own homes. "Fellowship" is the term used for this.

Amid the shouts and high fives (do folks high five at all churches?), the preacher wiped his forehead again and instructed us to turn to another passage. We quickly flipped to Proverbs, chapter 23, verse 20. It read, "Be not among drunkards, or among gluttonous eaters of meat." The sounds of the congregation intensified. This time, there was a lot more grunting than before. I noticed there seemed to also be more people "guilty" of what seemingly was "evil communications" than the first passage of Scripture had alluded to. See, in the sect of Christianity I grew up in, we believed in this thing called "holiness." Now, I do not want to confuse this with what is known as "Holiness" churches, because they are not exactly the same thing. But "holiness" for my church/branch of Christianity was to be "undefiled" by the things of the secular world. For many in my church, consuming alcohol was one of the things that could "defile" you. Additionally, being around those who defiled themselves with alcohol could make you just as guilty. I missed out on so many family functions due to this indoctrination. I avoided friend invitations to events for this same reason. I simply could not afford to be considered "unclean" before God. This understanding was something that ruined relationships and isolated believers, yet we were willing to pay the price of loneliness if it meant God would accept us. Occultist? Sure. But there we were.

As I took account of the congregation's reaction, the preacher began to turn the tables a bit. Suddenly, the passage of Scripture he was referring to was no longer about "others." No, it was about *us*. He began "calling us out." Some for drinking and most for being gluttonous eaters of meat. "It's clear! Some of you . . . some more than others, have been gluttonous!" He began to mimic the voice of a woman: "But Pastor, this is just baby fat." The congregation chuckled. "NO! You're thirty-five years old now!" He continued, again in the voice of the woman: "But Pastor, you know I'm big boned." "NO! No human has bones *THAT* big!" The congregation erupted in laughter. The louder the laughter became, the more I started to drop my head. The weight of my head almost seemed unbearable to lift. I wondered within myself if God had told him about me? I wonder if he was aware that I have been fat my whole life, and it was not because I eat a lot of meat? In that moment, I was aware that none of those things mattered. Fatness was being viewed through one lens, and that was the one of gluttony. I worked most of my adult life up to this point to be someone who followed God relentlessly. I had sacrificed more than I'd like to recall.

The preacher turned back to the microphone to throw one of his last daggers before the altar call. As he closed out his sermon, interweaving how we need to both work on ourselves and be mindful of the interactions we have with others, he spoke about gluttony one more time, stating, "And gluttony is as *IDOLA-TRY! We NEED God's MERCY!*" I felt myself go numb. Was my body the representation of sin in my life? I was so sure it wasn't that morning when I got ready for church. I was so sure I had been practicing self-control throughout the week. If thinness was to be equated to holiness, then perhaps this was why I had been slow to receive more money, a husband, or the blessings given by God so freely. The altar music had begun to play. I sighed inwardly from the depths of my soul. I had a decision to make. I saw so many people going to the altar. Not sure if this happens in other churches, but in Black churches, sometimes if you make eye contact with the person who is on their way for prayer, they will give you a look as to say, "What you waiting for?" so you too can join them. I knew there was not one person in the congregation that would not give me that look. In that moment, I was happy my head was so heavy. I was happy I could not see what anyone else was doing. Shame was resting in my mind, body, and soul. Sitting in my seat, I prayed that God would remove any of the gluttony I had hidden in my life. Maybe it was meat or maybe it was potatoes. Perhaps it was the mac and cheese I'm given the responsibility to make every Thanksgiving. Even worse, maybe it was not food at all! Was it possible that a fat body had been the punishment of the Lord because I was a glutton in some other part of my life?! The agony!

* * *

It has been long documented the relationship that the church has with larger bodies and food (Feeley-Harnik 1995). Food through the lens of religion takes on both literal and symbolic meaning. In her article on Christianity and eating disorders, Margaret Miles chronicles how individuals in the early church operated from the idea of "safe eating," scrutinizing what was consumed and how it was consumed (Miles 1995). Additionally, several scriptures in the Bible uphold similar standards, restricting the children of Israel from consuming certain meats (Leviticus 11:3, 7–8). It is also peculiar that Jesus often refers to himself as the bread of life, and instructs believers to drink of his blood and eat of his body (John 6:56). Lastly, as diet culture has expanded, so has its influence on the church. The Maker's Diet is one that is publicized, as participants only eat organic fruits and vegetables (Rubin 2013). Fasts such as the Daniel Fast are also encouraged during the beginning of each year to promote spiritual and bodily cleansing (Gregory 2010).

The idea that fat bodies emerged due to the overabundance of consumption is both fatphobic and simply not factual (Strings 2019). What's worse, there is no length that people are not willing to go to please a God they have never seen. Tying smaller bodies to the reward system man has created on earth only reinforces the idea that to be smaller is better. This is what we know today as modern healthism sans "God" (Crawford 1980). Anyone can be a partaker of this ideology and become a beneficiary of the good things in life. Is it that losing weight makes people happier, achieve more in their careers, and find the love they were always searching for? Or is it that we as a society have been conditioned to see larger bodies as less deserving, thus making it harder for them to enjoy the same things, advance in their careers, or find mates that will not be ridiculed for accepting them?

In his research, Parasecoli speaks to the ways that food intake is likened to what it means to be a follower of Christ (Parasecoli 2015). Within Christianity, there is great emphasis on self-control and being able to "master" your flesh or carnal nature, the thing that causes you to sin, which ultimately causes you to be an enemy of God. As a result, individuals who subscribe to this ideology are always seeking ways to deny themselves the pleasure that spills over into overindulgence. Simply put, to be a follower of Christianity is to dance like someone's watching. "Losing" yourself in worldly pleasure can mean that you also lose your place in heaven. One should have fun but not too much. One can be angry, but not to the point it leads to sin. One (read as *only* married couples) can orgasm, but if that orgasm makes you want to orgasm all the time, you are in trouble! If this sounds exhausting, that's because it is. Self-control is seen as a crux that Christians build their relationship with God on. And eating falls into this spectrum because ice cream, cake, chicken, collard greens, and cornbread are fucking delicious and, because of this fact, the body will not be able to control itself! I would roll my eyes harder as I type this, but then I would not be able to continue writing. I will say that like much of the assumptions written in biblical Scriptures about mankind and our tendencies to go astray from the perfect will of God, this notion also misses the mark for me. I, for one, believe that getting lost in the pleasures of life is, in fact, a pleasure and privilege of the living! By all means, allow your eyes to roll back in your head when the perfect bite of greens and mac and cheese comes together to speak to the lost places of your soul! That is a feeling you should not deny. For it is only by feeling this, and other emotions like anger, frustration, or bliss, that you can identify what's happening in your person. Feeling (both literally and metaphorically) is sometimes the only thing that signals we are still living (both literally and metaphorically).

When considering the emphasis on self-control in Christianity, it is no surprise that some of Parasecoli's results found that often the amount of food intake can be seen as sinful, particularly to those who are dieting, and how that consumption should be moderated by one's ability to have self-control. While this may seem somewhat innocent on the surface, the rhetoric does not take into account that moderation is subjective and will vary individually. Moreover, to tie food consumption to Scripture and approval from God also creates a power dynamic that thrusts individuals into dieting and disordered eating to appease a being that never actually speaks on their bodies. He instead uses His "messengers." Sabrina Strings talks about how this became problematic, especially for Black bodies (Strings 2019). Both lay members and clergy of the Protestant faith coupled the doctrine of healthism with racism to paint fat Black bodies as unkempt, lazy, and sinful. They were said to be consuming more than their fair share. They were seen as violators of God's Word and law. With this perspective, they could never be seen as acceptable. They would never qualify to be equal. And just like all the other components of White supremacy, this too would eventually infiltrate Black churches and spiritual ideologies.

A lack of respect for size diversity breeds an intolerance for others. It also then justifies ill-treatment of the people who are labeled "different." Very much like the preacher who exclaimed that being fat was because gluttony was at work, intolerance does not take the time to learn because it does not feel like it has to. What has been generalized to others does well because, well, it's the truth for those who practice it. It is more about forcing those who are labeled as "other" to fit into the box prescribed them. Hence, shaming. The idea of shame and stigma is to label and treat someone negatively, leaving them the option to change or endure. For those living in larger bodies, change is often a hard-fought, losing battle. And due to the lack of education of those who are making the rules, the punishment to endure is harsh and nonsensical. Fat people are denied basic access to things like seating, because if they really wanted to belong in a space, they'd do what is necessary to fit in. Christianity is not exempt from this, even as those who fill up the pews in most Black churches are fat Black women and men. Even in this space, these individuals chalk up their larger bodies to their own practices. They condemn themselves for the sake of the cross. They internalize the stigma and negative labels, believing that a certain type of body ought to be presented before God and others. And while the cleanliness of heart is what is to matter most to God, aesthetically speaking, a man and a woman should take care of themselves physically to attract one another and produce babies for the "Kingdom." Fat people are often left out of this conversation.

* * *

As the altar call and service ended, the congregation was reminded to remain and fellowship at the church dinner. I can't say that many were exuberant about eating after we had just been "cleansed" from our ungodly ways. Making our journey into the dining hall, we could smell fried chicken filling the halls. This type of smell had been created by a professional with a long standing in frying chicken. If you've ever been to a Black church dinner, you'll quickly learn that select people are asked to do certain things; making dishes is one of them (Harriot 2019). The type of smell that filled the hall suggested the temperature of the oil had to be just right. The closer we got, we could see that drumsticks, thighs, and breasts had the perfect golden-brown crust of seasoned flour. The sides table was full of mash potatoes, mac and cheese, green beans, cooked cabbage, and salad.

The dessert table had an assortment of cakes, cookies, and pies. To drink? Your choice of iced tea, water, or soda. Sometimes we had that drink where you mix the soda and sherbet, but that was only for special occasions.

As we made our way to seats, we waited for someone to come in and "bless" the food. After we said grace, the commotion began. Everyone up all at once, hoping the food tasted as good as it smelled. There were servers behind each station making sure no one was gluttonous in their choosing (also a norm in the Black church). You could absolutely revisit the table for more, but the servers behind the table were experts in negotiation during each visit and were sure not to give you more than they thought you deserved. As rounds were made and we all found our seats, fellowshipping commenced. Much laughter and enjoyment was spent around the consumption of the food we ate. A traditional staple in many Black families, food is the crux that brings us together and holds our attention long enough that we stay focused on one another (Hayford, n.d.). The crafting of meals is somewhat spiritual in itself. It teaches us to cook with the best ingredients to render a flavor that speaks to how we feel about one another. Food in Black culture is a conduit of communication. A feeling. A connection. And while soul food is often demonized in mainstream society as unhealthy, the spread in most Black families includes all food groups, cooked with different techniques according to a dish's need (Hayford, n.d.).

I think it's safe to say here that Black folk do not *only* eat food slathered in lard and butter. We do not *only* drink beverages that are so laden with sugar they taste like a lighter version of flavored syrup. That's also not all soul food. Considering a large number of Black people who reside in the United States are considered "overweight" or "obese" by the dubious BMI, assumptions are made that suggest these exaggerated versions of their diet are why. Yet, if one were to spend time in a Black community, it would quickly become evident that those who lead the charge in cooking family dinners include all food groups in meals when they can afford it. Poorer families may not have the same resources readily accessible to have fresh veggies, but they do their best with frozen or canned versions. And before people start to scream about canned vegetables not being "healthy": I get it. But I also get how folks have been fed lies for decades about using them. I also get that it costs thirty-three cents for a can of corn in some places. If I'm a parent who wants to incorporate some type of vegetable into the meal, and I'm planning for my family what I can afford, we're going to eat that thirty-three cent can of corn. This rule goes for all variations of vegetables or other foods. Boxed potatoes and shells and cheese easily come to mind here. A brisk walk through a local dollar store will show you the accessibility of these things at affordable prices versus whatever one can get at a farmers' market or local grocer.

I should also add: we do not need a replacement (hello, kale and quinoa!) for what is already present (Melton 2018). We do not want to lose our heritage based on assumptions about our consumption. Very much as in other collectivist cultures, food is a part of our identity. We are not interested in depleting other cultures of their food sources because Europeans have just discovered the joy and flavor of avocado toast. We have our own flavors that have been nurtured for centuries (African American Registry, n.d.). There is no need to give that up. Yet, like previously discussed, when a majority labels a group as "other," much is not discussed about their needs. No one is concerned about what is being lost. Change is the order of the day. The pressure is on to see that the perspective of the majority be taken up and implemented.

I would sit through several reiterations of gluttony, getting in shape to preach the Gospel, and rhetoric that included how eating better should be considered when preparing for a husband before my departure from the church in 2014. Looking back, it saddens me to know that I allowed myself to be talked to and about in such a way that was not reflective of my habits or my history with food. The pressure of healthism and Christianity created a new meaning regarding food intake that would take some time to undo. The chastisement that came from the pulpit coupled with the extravagant meals that followed after also left me confused. If food was an avenue we used to express ourselves in love, what was to be said about the servers who gave you what they *thought* you should have? What does it say about the way we prepare our meals and who we choose to share them with? Were these things taken into account when the sermons and weight loss programs were being formed? My guess would be: no.

Spending roughly thirteen years heavily involved in church ministry taught me a few things that I think are worth sharing related to food, bodies, and care. I cannot, nor do I desire to, speak for all Black churches, but this is my experience and I think it is a worthwhile critique because so many of us in the community come in contact with the church in this variation throughout our lifetimes. I hope to speak to those who have experienced similar treatment, standing in solidarity and validating your experience. To be a landmark for the Black community moving forward, the church should be mindful of the experiences of others. I am grateful to have survived through the turmoil of fat talk and shame, among other things, but I'm aware that not everyone does. Just as those living in marginalized populations *within* the Black community are not shielded from the mistreatment at the hands of church leadership that is informed through mainstream societal views, those in leadership positions are not shielded from perpetuating that bias. For clarification, "fat talk" is defined as talk around fat on bodies irrespective of the context. It can be explicit like someone saying that they hate the fat on their bodies, or less intrusive like someone complimenting the looks of another while simultaneously stating that they wish their body looked smaller like the person they are using as a comparison.

For many people who seek out churches and find comfort there, the institution is seen as a "home" of sorts. A place where dwellers are supposed to be safe. What I learned from my experience was that fat bodies were not. In fact, they were the antithesis of what a godly body should represent. Dressing modestly meant something different for me. Where others could wear a skirt right above the knee, I could not, because I had "more" (more knee, I suppose) to cover. Blouses on me could not be fitted. T-shirts had to be twice as long to cover my hips and butt. While I was appreciated for my service, I was not considered to be good-looking or to qualify as marriage material. I, in short, was a mammy.

Most fat women I came across also spent time in the kitchen with the food. These women were matriarchs of their families and used their time and effort to produce meals out of love. They found honor in being able to provide families with sustenance. Within their fingers, they possessed the legacies of life that oozed strategy about unity. Well-prepared food could bring folks to the table to negotiate around matters of collective action. Can you imagine the number of protests, revolts, and resistance plans discussed over pound cake and grilled fish?! Well-prepared food was also the farewell gift in seeing loved ones off on long journeys that they may never return from. It was a "last supper" of sorts for many. These women were healers in so many unspoken ways, and although at least on the periphery the appreciation for this was noted, in the same breath our bodies were seen as offensive as they related to Scripture. Somehow, with all the love and mindfulness we carried toward the Lord, we missed this glaring issue of gluttony that we just could not seem to break.

I have been in congregations where people have given God praise because they were sick and lost weight as a result. This weight loss was explained as a blessing from the Lord, with no explanation as to the sickness. The weight loss was also expected to remain, while the sickness was not. People were told that the weight would stay off. However, as their bodies recovered, so did their weight gain. And just like that, they were the problematic gluttons again.

The Bible is clear when it says that the people of God perish for a lack of knowledge (Hosea 4:6). Considering this, one would hope that the Scripture here would be applied to all things and not just the Bible. Understanding that fatphobia runs rampant in our society, it would behoove those who assert that what they hear is from God to determine if it's not simply their own words. Gluttony is not *the* reason for fatness. Genetics matters, and body diversity is okay.

By utilizing the rubric of healthism and supporting it through Scripture, the Black church has also been used as a tool to continue the practices used to deem fat Black members unacceptable via the racist Protestant rules of old. This, in turn, leaves those in fat bodies to question if God has a bone to pick with us, or if church leadership is simply lacking in their awareness, two options that both have consequences. I came across a video circulating on the internet about a year or so ago and found women praying and casting out fatness and "spirits" that caused this "problem." If this is how some feel about their own bodies and I am bigger than they are, how can it be ensured that care for me and my body is fostered in an environment that repeatedly has preached the same message?

TENSIONS IN SPIRITUALITY AND HOW TO CO-EXIST

Spirituality can be a touchy subject when groups historically condemned confront these ideologies held by the majority. It was great to have guests on the podcast who chronicled their journey of body acceptance while holding their spiritual beliefs intact.

Malaika Salaam of Purple Hair and Converse visited the podcast to talk in great detail about her spirituality and the impact it has had on all the work she does as a fat Black femme. For her, she had a grandmother who helped guide her path and lead her to the place of understanding how spirituality would be a driving force in her life: "I remember being seven years old and her pulling me aside and trying to explain this gift I had . . . this thing that she saw in me. . . . The people who hold on to that [revelation] through life and their experiences are the ones who become the 'hope dealers.' All of us were given these gifts. Whether you choose to cultivate them, whether you choose to ignore them, all of that becomes based on how you engage the world."

Confidence coach Erica Ware also attributed her choice to get involved in affirming women to her spirituality and gifting. During her time on the podcast, she spoke about her ability to overcome obstacles and about knowing there was a greater purpose fueling her decision making. She also discussed how she used her spirituality as a way to channel this hope in others: "The fact that I'm a Black fat woman, and not only am I fat, but I'm 'superfat.' I'm a whopping size 26, 28, sometimes 30, and there are no other women in my industry who are my size who are actually speaking life into other women. That alone leaves a lasting impression on people, because when I open my mouth, they're not expecting me to say that I am a mind-transformation or confidence coach. So, my existence alone is super impactful."

Spirituality in this sense has acted as fuel or encouragement in allowing those who reside in a fat Black body to do what they do, but it takes a breaking away from mainstream ideas of what spirituality is and how it functions for its believers.

DOCTORS AND THEIR
DAMN RECOMMENDATIONS

"Come on over to the scale and let's get you weighed," she said. Trotting on that cold tiled floor, I stood on the scale awaiting both the number and the moral value that accompanied it. I hated doctors' offices. I hated how nurses listened to my story and then jotted down whatever they believed were my issues. I always remember how the metal piece of the mechanical scale would clunk to the bottom when I stood on the platform. Throughout the years, that annoyance became a sense of relief, because I would always tell myself the clunk that I heard was cool because the nurse needed to still adjust the rest. In my mind, the weighing hadn't even begun yet. In my mind, that meant there was room for redemption. The next set of clunks would vary based on my age. When I was ten to twelve, maybe three was about right. Fifty pounds for each, I believe. I would stand fidgeting with my hands, staring at the fluorescent lights, and staring at the posters on the wall that always talked about some illness or disease I did not have. I wondered how long it would take to get that metal piece in the middle of the scale to stay balanced, not swinging too high or low.

The nurse's index finger would appear, inching the pound mechanism of the scale to the right. I would stare at the balance intently, hoping and sometimes even praying that it would hold steady in the middle. Sometimes it would, but other times, that little finger would push the pound counter so far to the right, I would roll my eyes knowing that the nurse could've just moved to the next set of 50 pounds to make my life easier. As I got older, I started to speak up ahead of time, telling them they would have to move it. I did it with a smile on my face. They never took my word for it. After I stepped off the scale with a report of weight down to the ounce, the nurse would never say much. I'd lift myself onto the examining bed, ripping the tissue paper and adjusting myself as I waited to speak to the doctor.

"We really gotta do something about this weight." "You can make little changes and see a difference." "Have you been tested for diabetes?" All these recommendations for a sinus infection. All these recommendations AFTER my blood work comes back good. All these recommendations despite me expressing that I am active and am mindful of the things I eat. And what do they mean when they say, *"we"*?! *We* would not be eating cauliflower rice. *We* also would not be deciding where an additional $30–$45 a month would come from to join a gym, buy new workout clothes, or afford kale chips and cauliflower rice!

Tuh! Healthism was literally impeding my health, and fatphobia was the vehicle it was riding in (Bacon and Severson 2019). Sure, most health professionals would never say that they hate their patients, but there was a certain sting I felt as they talked about weight, fat, and my health. I sensed that there was a general consensus that no one, no woman, should want to weigh what I did. The ways their eyes would drop, as though I should have felt sorry to be in the body I was in, told a story that I was doomed. The sharpness of their tone when they told me I needed to make a change immediately or my health would start to decline spoke of a hatred they had for fat and that it was seen as an enemy. Days sitting in those offices biting my tongue were rough!

Rough, and at times hard to detect where the discontentment and hatred were *really* coming from.

Healthism can be defined as ascribed moral uprightness and personal achievement attributed to physical fitness and nutrition (Crawford 1980). To add, it can also be defined as bullshit. Healthism is not a new concept, yet it is one that has been repurposed over decades. If anyone has ever watched an episode of *The Biggest Loser* or *My 600 lb. Life*, they should be fully aware of the ways that personal achievement is attached to smaller bodies. Despite the information that has been revealed about both shows and dieting, oddly it does not stop the general public from believing these falsehoods. Moreover, health professionals are not exempt (although some argue that they should be) from this inundation of pseudo facts. The visceral reaction toward my body in the offices of doctors stems from the fatphobia served to America on a silver platter. That I can be both fat and healthy is a truth most medical professionals are unwilling to wrap their minds around (Phelan et al. 2015). In fact, it is these very notions that have been recorded in research and news articles throughout the country. Health professionals blame patients for the outcome of their weight; and because they see higher weights as negative, they in turn treat the patient negatively. These are individuals with access to research, and the resources to conduct their own research, stuck in a mirage of Keto Diet outcomes, believing that Weight Watchers is really about wellness and not weight loss. Some of the biggest peddlers of healthism reside in the health care industry. Doctors are not immune.

In my own research of *The Biggest Loser* and *My 600 lb. Life*, participants often likened their ability to have a love life (despite being married), a career, or a relationship with their children to weight loss. In all of their scenarios, it was fat that made them a morally bankrupt or an unattractive person (Cox 2018). On the show *My 600 lb. Life*, participants often referred to themselves as "monsters." They saw their bodies as not human. Fat had disqualified them from having a life they could enjoy, or at least enjoy without feeling bad about it. Participants on *The Biggest Loser* had similar tales, yet missed that MOST if not all of the activities they participated in, they did so in larger bodies. Every challenge was done in fat bodies. Hours in the gym? Spent in a fat body.

I knew at some point if I did not find a voice to speak up for myself, *even* if I was also watching intently that middle scale balance, that I would be railroaded and bombarded with a bunch of information about my body and my worth that would not fare well for me mentally or emotionally. The first time I blurted out in the doctor's office that I would "lose weight when I get ready!" I was roughly twelve years old. Frightened and fed up, I did so because I felt like I had no other choice. After voicing my thoughts, I realized that I had indeed also made a choice. In that moment, I declared to accept my body as it was, and I vowed to *only* change it when I was ready. Fuck the doctors and their recommendations! My dimpled thighs and I had found a voice!

Part 2

To Accept
Is to Resist

3

TO ACCEPT AND
BE ACCEPTED

*T*imes of acceptance have been present yet fleeting throughout my life. According to the dictionary, acceptance is defined as the action of consenting to receive or undertake something offered; the action or process of being received as adequate or suitable, typically to be admitted into a group; or agreement with or belief in an idea, opinion, or explanation. It's really interesting that the definition can be in the context of receiving or being received. In my life, on both ends of this spectrum, I have learned to receive and accept my body, honoring it for all it does and how it presents. For example, there was that one time in first grade when I was a duckling in the *Ugly Duckling* play. I felt so tall in my bright yellow leotard! I had yellow stockings to match. My hair was pressed, full of body and curled at the end. My body felt like it fit. Fit into what exactly, I do not know, but none of me felt out of place. The leotard was made for me. The stockings, shoes, and ribbons too. I had no speaking role in the play, but I was a viable member of that duckling family and there was *no one* that could tell me different!

Then there was the moment when I noticed I had identical dimples on the side of my thighs. Looking back, I envision the clear skies and can hear the faint chirps of birds in the background. Pretty sure I was in the fifth grade by then. By that time, I was somewhat aware of the fact that a body like mine had "flaws" compared to my classmates. Often I was seen as simply round with no definition. But in that moment, as I traced my fingers across the small indentations on my outer thighs, feeling them dip simultaneously in the same space, I smiled in contentment. Even if everyone else only saw me as round, I knew that curves and dips in my body existed and that they were special. I played with those dimples incessantly. I made sure to check and see if they were still present day after day, year after year. Those little pockets of sanctuary reminded me daily that I was special and helped me to accept that skin didn't have to be smooth to be beautiful. I held on tight to the tenderness of my palms and the one beauty mark on my right hand. I loved the way my hair curled without effort. I appreciated the almond shape of my eyes. Occasionally, I caught a glimpse of my silhouette in the mirror and saw the beauty in it. But that was occasionally. Sometimes the occasion included shapewear. Most of the time the occasion included shapewear. Pretty sure, I tried on my first girdle at the age of ten. They were the panties with the zigzag stitched panel in the front. I can't remember exactly where I got it from, but I wanted to know what all the hype of having a smoother (which I thought at the time equated to a smaller) belly was all about. Spoiler alert: those panties did not make my stomach smaller! Instead, they cut the circulation off in my thighs! Thick welted red marks would rest in the crevices of my skin long after those undies were removed. Again, I questioned, what was so special about having a flat tummy? It did seem to go away when I lay on my back, but then I couldn't move, and what was the fun in that?! It also wasn't fun to make drum noises on like I'd done with my larger belly before. I did, however, notice that having a flat tummy did give you freedom.

If your stomach was flat, you could wear short shirts like Winnie-the-Pooh. Oddly enough, Pooh wore his short shirt despite having a round tummy. Something older folk still have trouble explaining. You also had a better choice in clothing. Fun colors. Nothing with little flowers everywhere. People with flat stomachs also seemed to generally be liked more. It didn't matter if they were *actually* nice people. Thinness gave individuals a favor not afforded to larger kids. No, we were considered lazy, clumsy, and slow. No one wanted to see our bellies in short shirts. No one bothered to learn if we were *actually* nice.

With such a large body for my age, acceptance equated to making concerted efforts to show myself working toward losing weight. And when I wasn't working toward this, I should at least be talking about how I would like to. Another thing was that outings should include layers. Layers of shirts, jackets, sweaters, and anything else that would suggest my body could be hidden. In reality, I knew it couldn't; but again, it was more about acknowledging that it did not deserve to be seen. I was being conditioned to be invisible. The size of my body rendered this judgment without my input.

By the time I started to garner a voice for myself, I had almost a decade of fat talk and stigma pressing against me. Stepping out in revealing clothes (by revealing, I mean one layer) would be a challenge. It made me nauseous to consider publicly appreciating the pieces of my body I admired in the dark. Finally turning to family members and saying that I didn't care what they thought of my body was a long time coming. But I did it in my own way. And when I did, all hell broke loose! I was laughed at more. Criticized more. My appreciations were not seen as great feats to others. I realized that a war had been waged against me that had no intentions of slowing down whether I chose to speak or not. So I kept speaking.

By internalizing previous fatphobic messages and treatment that blamed me for my body, I had twice the amount of work to do. Alone, I unpacked the lies I believed about myself. I looked my body over in the mirror and normalized what it meant to live in my skin. I sat down and ran my fingers across the dimples on my thighs. I reminded myself that my body is a vehicle, a vehicle that has done right by me most of the days I have been breathing. I've loved in it. Cried in it. Ate pizza and ice cream, and pretzels, and broccoli in it. It was and still is my hero.

Externally, I learned to pick my battles. I stopped sitting at tables (both literally and figuratively) when people began to loathe their own bodies. I decided to share my truth about the ill-treatment I received due to my size. I did research to better understand that the hatred toward fat bodies is systemic and is really against all bodies if a dollar can be made (Bacon and Severson 2019). Fat and marginalized folks just bear the brunt of the sword.

To me, general acceptance was possible but temporary. Body acceptance was rare. So rare that when others did accept my body, I had a hard time finding what to do with that information. I chose not to believe them despite their compliments making me feel validated. I rejected romantic advances, believing the nudges and microaggressions I had heard most of my life. Whispers filled my mind repeating the critiques of yesteryear. Could I find someone who would accept me *and* my stretched belly? Was I really trying my best or just being lazy?

My first few journeys in acceptance would be taken alone. And they would not be the flowery imagination I had in my head. No, I was not setting doctors' offices and institutions ablaze, tearing down fat hate, and changing policies based on the research I read. At times, I was struggling to even find the right things to say to doctors to convey my beliefs.

In the beginning, acceptance felt like anger when doctors still refused to see past my weight to render a needed diagnosis for care. It also felt like comfort in times of mourning when I wasn't picked . . . for anything. Because as I began to learn, rejection in a larger body was common for everything. From romance to working with partners for a school project, being the fat kid and being appealing, popular, or any other type of positive word in the English lexicon was an oxymoron. However, rejection *because* of acceptance was something different. This was me making a choice first. It was me drawing the line in the sand about what I would and would not accept. I had been called to table to negotiate the terms of my existence and decided "No deal!" It was empowering. I had inadvertently provoked rejection by changing the narrative of my identity I once had no agency in.

I can remember being accepted more for my skills and personality as opposed to the whole "package," which included what those skills and personality came in. People were always calling on me to do tasks. Did those who laughed at my jokes defend me when jokes were made about my appearance? Did they make sure to check accommodations for someone my size when considering trips or outings? What about diet talk . . . did that cease? Hmm. Granted, all encounters were not bad. I always had a small circle, more like a triangle, of friends who never made me feel out of place for being the biggest in the group. There was encouragement for me to wear *whatever* I wanted. I danced with them. Celebrated with them. We still communicate to this day.

When I found community online, understanding the nuances of acceptance highlighted the difference between acceptance and inclusion. For so long, I thought acceptance was *acceptance*.

Like, if I was invited to the party, I was accepted, end of story. But what I quickly learned was that it was one thing to be invited, and another to arrive only to find chairs that could not bear the weight of my thighs, or to find that the venue is full of individuals who hate their bodies and are offended that you do not hate yours too. I needed to be at venues and hear "yassssss" or "ayyyyyyyyeeee" when "Back That Thang Up" came on and we hit the dance floor to take over for the '99 & 2000. I needed to trust that I wasn't going to have to contort my body into a seat or booth to enjoy dinner out with friends. I needed to know I was fully accepted.

It's interesting how acceptance works from the other side. It requires concerted effort on the part of the ignorant to be informed and make changes accordingly. As a cisgender woman, if I want to ensure that my LGBTQ+ sisters are accepted in my circles, I gotta learn about them. I gotta be willing to spend time with them and listen. And while we may have much in common on this fat life path, when it comes to their lived experience as queer, I buckle up and prepare to get schooled. I hold space for them, listening intently for the access they need. Acceptance isn't hard when it's done intently. It isn't hard when it's done with care. Half-assed acceptance is where the majority of all mishaps happen because it was, well, half-assed. I'm always slightly taken aback to hear people who I thought were fully accepting of me be clueless as to the struggles I face living in a larger body. I wonder who I was telling my story to all this time. They wonder when did I start being mistreated because of the size of my body. They gasp and look in disbelief when I tell them about my doctor visits. And sometimes, it is that same gasp and disbelief I see in their eyes as they seek to grasp empathy for a situation they have no knowledge about.

Their hearts seek and search to relate to a situation they themselves have never had to live through. Sometimes I stop and tell them that it's okay if they can't relate. Acceptance doesn't mean you always have to fight. It can be soft and very much a matter of fact. They can simply sit with the truths they've just been told and accept them as such, because it is what it is.

Up until this point, I had a pretty good grasp on what it meant to go where I'm celebrated. For me, fat acceptance is a tool of empowerment for a number of reasons. Primarily because by accepting, we also subsequently empower and give back dignity (Hampton 2018). In order to navigate this world as a member of marginalized groups, you need strategy. The concept of fat acceptance provides this for those who embrace it by giving space to unpack the things we were taught to be fearful of and avoid (Hampton 2018). How can one address the beauty in their belly if they are constantly running from its reflection in the mirror? How can one advocate for better practices in the health care field if they are not first accepting that they are receiving subpar treatment?

Much of what I now practice to maintain body peace and liberation comes from the endless hours of unpacking my own fatphobia, anti-Black ideas, and internalized weight stigma. For years I was mean to myself. I did not think I deserved the best. I did not see my voice as valuable. I allowed myself to be pushed out of the way for promotion and recognition because of my own qualms. I avoided certain items of clothing and bright colors. I attempted to shrink my body in hopes of fitting into spaces that were never designed for me to be in. Unpacking hurt, but it also healed. With every makeshift band-aid of faux confidence and self-esteem I removed, a true genuine scab of body appreciation formed. Soon I was no longer worried about remaining invisible. I started to wear what I wanted, pressing past the ideas of what others might think. I was loud when I laughed. I stopped code-switching as much. I found the voice to say what I wanted and to advocate for what I needed. I was a shiny, sparkling diamond

of Black fatness! I was accepting myself. I was open to the possibilities of what could come next. That tall emotional wall I
had built was slowly starting to crumble. At least that's what I
thought.

I met Sam online in the summer of 2013 while studying at
the University of Missouri–Columbia. Having been well versed
in the "You'll never get a man at the size you are" rhetoric, I was
extremely hesitant and skeptical about what his true interest in
me could be. I mean, I was well aware that I had stunning skills
and a sparkling personality, but as I mentioned before, finding
someone who wanted the "package" was quite a feat. And when
I say, someone who wanted the "package," I'm not speaking of
my body in terms of objectification.

There is no shortage of individuals, particularly in my case,
cisgender men, who fetishize fat women. For those who are into
the sport of finding and sleeping with fat people, "hogging" is
the term (Yeboah 2019). In fact, there is no shortage of cisgender men who will have sex with fat women . . . in private. I had
previously come across these scenarios, adding credence to the
rhetoric of what it means to be fat and undatable. On some level,
I grew to believe these things, and as the conversation between
Sam and me intensified, I went back over these thoughts in my
mind to ensure I had left nothing hidden that would posit him to
be taken back by the size of my body.

When he sent messages about my physique, I would go back
to the pictures to ensure that my full body was visible. Staring
intently at the picture I had stared at intently before I had shared
it, I'd check. Face? Check. Waist? Check. Hips facing forward?
Yep, got it. Why? Because there was so much talk about men
feeling like fat women had been catfishing them after they met
them in person. I roll my eyes at this notion and count it as
bullshit, but also would not dare not to double-check that I was
in the clear. As a form of precaution, it was best to let a man

see me from my head to my toes to know that (1) I was not a size 2, and (2) to some degree, I also had fat toes if they were wondering. In short, online dating was a chore! To put yourself on display in hopes of being accepted by people without the security blanket of them knowing your skill set or being exposed to your personality was terrifying. For so much of my life, I had been told that I was such a nice person, or funny, or a great team player. Now to be judged by appearance, an appearance already rejected in mainstream society, my guard was way up. How are fat bodies supposed to convey all the great things we possess if people will not spend enough time on our profiles to learn about them? Moreover, to be Black and fat comes with even more barriers, as Black women are one of the least desirable groups in online dating (Meyer 2018). As a fat Black woman, the extra step needed to be fully transparent was just another barrier to finding acceptance among a pool of participants who have been told narratives about me before hearing my personal story.

Talks with Sam grew longer and more frequent. He was interested in my life and wanted to know about my plans for the future. His favorite feature of me was my smile. I was smitten. By August we had officially become a couple and made plans to meet in November. Reluctant to share details with my family, I kept our relationship a secret until my trip to Pennsylvania for Thanksgiving. I needed to ward off the negativity of dating someone online and the question of "Does he know what you look like?" I needed to not think of the possibility of Sam seeing me and deciding that by some stretch of his imagination he was catfished by the fat girl living in Missouri who couldn't be honest. No, I just wanted to go and meet him for myself without any outside voices. I wanted to see what it might be like to have someone *accept* me. All the days of turning men down and brushing off microaggressions from outsiders had come to a head in my decision to meet Sam. In my quiet time, I was realizing that I wasn't as good at brushing these things off as I thought. Gosh, I hoped he liked me! I didn't want to return from this meetup disappointed and single. I didn't want what research states, that fat people are less likely to build interpersonal bonds romantically, to be true. I also didn't want to be discouraged or put off by others' opinions. It took me twelve hours to drive from Missouri to Pennsylvania to New York City, but the thirty minutes I had to wait to meet Sam after arriving at my hotel (he was late!) seemed like forever.

There I stood in the mirror checking myself out. I looked good! Hotels have some of the best mirrors. My hair was pressed. The leather patches of my sweater lay gently on my thighs. As I stood, I whispered affirmations: "You got this!" "Don't be nervous." "Is he even coming?" Sam was late and underground with no service. I felt hope leave my body with every minute that passed. When my phone finally lit up, I thought my lunch would take flight out of my belly as well. When I opened the door to greet him, I had never, ever, EVER seen a smile as bright as his! As we embraced, I felt happiness as well as relief. He didn't pull back from me and say he had been catfished. He didn't look for a way to leave immediately. He sat down and made himself comfortable. We took pictures. He stuck around.

Experiencing Sam's acceptance was an eye-opening experience. So much of what I thought I had put behind me was conjured up with his presence. I wondered what someone like him could see in someone like me, skills and personality aside. For reference, Sam was a few years younger than me. He was tall(er), dark, and handsome. His body was chiseled. There really was no place on his body where his muscles did not feature themselves. In presentation, he was someone who is typically considered "out of my league." This point was never made so clear than the time we both traveled to the post office to mail a package. Imagine walking into a place with your partner, conversing with them as you wait to be serviced, standing beside them as the service is being rendered, and being asked if there was something you could be helped with as though you entered the facility on your own. After I explicitly stated that Sam and I were together, the clerk's unlimited dispensary of tape and flirtatious behaviors seized up. Suddenly, her face changed as to communicate "Oh hell no!" and Sam's package was taped enough to be shipped. I smiled at her as our eyes met, knowing I had just ruined whatever fabricated reality she had formulated about Sam. I also did it as a sign to show that yes, I can be fat and described as inadequate to some while still being considered more than suitable to others. In that moment, I held the realities of acceptance and rejection in the same space. She was pissed, I was vindicated, and Sam, well Sam was clueless! Sam and I walked back to the car both feeling accomplished but obviously for different reasons.

There were times I pondered whether Sam really knew just how fat I was. Day after day, weekend after weekend, he reminded me that he did. I never told him I had these questions, but his acceptance reassured me that I was in the right place. I remember reading over Jes Baker's piece titled "Things No One Will Tell Fat Girls . . . So I Will" and being shocked that I wasn't the only one who thought this (Baker 2017). I mean, really, how could someone who chooses you daily not know?! Sounds silly now, but when vulnerability creeps into your life, you are not always prepared for what it exposes. You're not prepared to deal with the hurts of your childhood, the trauma of your adolescence, and the rejection you use as a weapon for protection as an adult. Being with Sam felt right, but it also awakened places in me I had to deal with if I wanted peace and to avoid self-sabotage. Being with him felt like hot chocolate and marshmallows in front of the fireplace (I don't think I've been in front of a fireplace either) in brand-new pajamas. It felt like sitting in your favorite chair that enveloped your body in microfiber, with the quality heavy blankets only grandparents buy to keep you warm. It felt like home. Our relationship brought to light what it meant to co-exist in the reality of another. Just like when I looked in that mirror in the hotel, I was able to look at Sam and see my reflection. Sam was a talking mirror too! At times I would look at him and he would tell me what he saw, which helped to shape and reinforce my identity. There was such vulnerability and safety. We had created a world where we spoke the same language, and I never had to be ashamed. There was no war to be fought in our chamber, but that didn't mean that battles disappeared.

ACCEPTANCE IS BLISSFUL

To find your people is a wonderful feeling. To find yourself is even better. I had the opportunity to sit down with a few guests of my podcast over the years who demonstrate the power of acceptance and how it fuels them to continue to thrive in both their personal and professional lives.

One of my most memorable guests was Ro'Yale, Da Queen of Curves. Ro'Yale is a plus-size pole dancer who went viral based off small documentary films about her involvement in the pole dancing industry. When I sat down with Ro'Yale, she spoke about her journey to body acceptance and what it meant to have the acceptance of others. In the case of instructing, she talked about how her presence is a factor in how she teaches. "With someone like me of size as an instructor, that lets that guard down for them [students who attend classes], and that allows them to hear what I'm saying aloud, and to be a better performer."

Concerning acceptance from others, Ro'Yale spoke about having the support of family and friends. She also detailed how this is not always the case and why she is grateful to have the support she has. "There are so many 'polers' who are like the greatest. . . . We call them 'polebrities.' And every now and then on Facebook they come on. And if they post something, it's like their mom will come on and say, 'I can't stand you doing that.'"

Ro'Yale wasn't alone in embracing acceptance. Author Cecily Alexandria visited the show to talk about body acceptance and her book that deals with the pressures of dating while being a virgin. During the show, Cecily spoke about the realization she had while participating in online dating of accepting herself and what it was like to see that others could accept her too. "When it came to dating, I was like, 'Oh! People can like me. I don't have to be super thin or look a certain way.' . . . I definitely had some real messed-up views of myself and just what was acceptable for a Black woman and a woman that was of a certain size."

Through both of these excerpts, it's clear to see that acceptance can be a catapult into changing mindsets and lives. Acceptance helps everyone and allows us to be fully ourselves.

4

ACCEPTANCE IS CHOOSING SIDES

Perhaps what the definition of acceptance doesn't lay out is the fact that typically when one accepts something, they also reject competing forces. For example, by me accepting my body "as is," I also rejected the notion that it needed to be changed. I pushed against all the other ideas and opinions that told me my body was not good enough. The definition of rejection is pretty straightforward. It means to dismiss or refuse a proposal, idea, etc. For me, I really enjoyed one of the synonyms of the word: "no." That's it. Short and simple. When someone contests the acceptance of my body in society, I simply say "No" and follow it with a broader explanation. "You're not fat, you're beautiful." No, I'm both! While rejection is typically seen as the opposite of acceptance, in my own experience, I've found that resistance is a better antonym because it denotes ongoing tensions, something that fat folk inevitably face. With every new diet, new explanation of fat people using more than their fair share of energy in the world, and new jackasses who think they're clever by recycling fat jokes, resistance becomes the call of the day. There is *always* a constant push and pull as it relates to progress in fat communities (Cox 2018). As we gain more access to clothing, a new fight ascends in health care. As we win small victories in occupation legislation, wellness apps develop predatory practices to capture our youth. Every day, those in the fat community show up to stand against the verbal and behavioral daggers thrown at us. What's probably more telling is the fact that just by showing up, we're also choosing sides and agitating opponents we didn't know we had. So, what is to be said about the complexities that rest in acceptance? Are fat people signing up for battle when they choose to accept their bodies and the fat bodies of others? Seems that way.

In my own research of status posts on Facebook, I found that fat people asserting acceptance for their bodies were often met with disdain from others in the comment section (Cox 2018). Commenters in opposition used communicative tactics that included gaslighting to "inform" status posters that the way they experienced the world in their body was inaccurate (i.e., "It's all in your head"). Status posters were then accused of being overly sensitive or labeled as "leftists" or "snowflakes." On my Instagram page, *Fresh Out the Cocoon,* I am often confronted by trolls who see my page as a platform on which they can argue their views to contest the content I post around fat liberation. For me, fat liberation is about larger bodies being given equitable access to resources and respect to exist in the bodies they have. I post content around these ideas, which include fat people loving and enjoying life. Additionally, I also include content that challenges diet culture and what we know about exercise, weight, and weight loss. I regularly use my platform to amplify the voices of other activists doing work in fat liberation and body diversity, especially if they are Black and fat.

To date, I have over 200 accounts blocked from my Instagram page. Simple posts that read "Fat is Sexy" have received hateful comments that I had to remove because people have shown up on my page, uninvited, to fat-shame and debate. Moreover, some people have gone to great lengths by sending private messages telling me that I should delete my page because I am promoting "obesity" or inaccurate information about fat and the body.

To be clear, I asked for none of this, but I did choose to accept. I chose to accept bodies that look like mine. I chose to accept that previous research on the harm that fat does to the body was misguided, used small nonrepresentative samples, and drew conclusions that were later disputed. By signing up for acceptance, I also signed up for resistance, even if it was in my ignorance. Signing up for acceptance put me in opposition to those who accepted all that I had rejected. This meant war. And war is not just prevalent outside of the community. No, to my sarcastic surprise, choosing to validate and value fat Black bodies also meant that I'd be facing war *within* the fat acceptance community among my White counterparts.

Fat White women draped in Black culture aesthetics. Fat White women using African American vernacular. Fat White women shedding White women tears after being called out for appropriation and a lack of education as it relates to the Black experience. Wash, rinse, repeat. This has primarily been my experience in White-dominated spaces. If White women are not trying to be more like us, they are grossly ignorant about what it means to know us. ALL of us. I'm not sure how long it took me to realize that a lot of what I watched White people do in their spaces of "inclusion" was parroting. Everyone knows how to confess that they have privilege. Very few, if any, know how to live a life that reflects such.

In "Fat People of Color: Emergent Intersectional Discourse Online," Apryl Williams highlights this very thing, citing the erasure of fat Black folk from fat activist spaces (A. A. Williams 2017). Previous research done by Michaela Ann Null also speaks to fat activism's intersectionality problem, noting it as a movement that is both overly heterosexual and White (Null 2012). In interviews, I found that many fat Black respondents felt the pressure to choose between being Black and being fat (Cox 2018). A choice that they should never have to make. After all, no one *ever* asks White people to choose. The hoops fat Black folk are presented with in order to belong to groups that highlight ONE aspect of their identity are daunting. It is also foolish to think that this identity can be separated from our lived experiences being Black. Similar to what Kimberlé Crenshaw found in her seminal research on intersectionality, the fat Black experience is a different one altogether due to the added oppression received because of an identity not found in the White/European experience (Crenshaw 1989). We live different. We rejoice different. We mourn different. We are not the same. It is insulting when one thinks with a change of attire and vernacular, they could relate. Even worse, if they feel like because they are sexually active with a Black partner, they'd be our equals. What we have, others cannot obtain by proximity.

What's so hard about learning, people? Is it really that difficult to reach across the table and start to build real relationships? I often ponder these questions because White folk make it seem so hard and awkward. It seems that they'd rather costume and then sit and listen. And perhaps it's the unpacking that makes sitting and listening hard (DiAngelo and Dyson 2018). Hearing your reflection through the view of others can be far worse than looking in the mirror and seeing yourself. You squirm and look for relief. You seek to justify and explain away what you see differently. Tears are shed in frustration. Tears are used as a tool to stop the synopsis. What is this notion that prevents them from deferring to those in the room who actually live the experience they're talking about? The entitlement to explain and justify poor explanations prevalent in White-dominated spaces makes clear that the fat Black experience is devalued. Even in their ignorance, White people believe they can teach it, wear it, and say it, better than we can. They lie. They lie and are delusional to that end. Whitesplaining is a thing, y'all. It's a thing and it's exhausting. Yet, just as my research shows, White people would rather disappear from the internet and block followers before they change, especially from the correction of a solely Black crowd (hey, Rebel!) (DiAngelo and Dyson 2018).

Acceptance. The action of consenting to receive something offered. The action or process of being received as adequate. The admittance into a group, or agreement with an explanation. Acceptance of the fat Black experience was and still is met with resistance. Acceptance of the fat Black queer experience was and still is met with resistance. What would it take to change the narrative? What if folks just stop giving a shit about being accepted and create a lane of their own?

AT SOME POINT, WE ALL CHOOSE SIDES

To date, there hasn't been one guest on my podcast that has not detailed what choosing sides has cost them. Whether it was constant gaslighting from family or loved ones, relationship loss, friendship departures, or the loss of material goods, there is a consequence incurred for going against the grain. The guests were no strangers to loss due to their belief in fat acceptance. They also were all too familiar with what it meant in choosing to also be clear that they identified as Black unapologetically. Malaika Salaam summed up this balance perfectly when she visited the podcast on spirituality: "You look at me and you can gauge that I am Black. The way that people like to frame it is to say, 'Oh you know she's a plus-size girl' or 'She's a big girl.' I like to use the word fat! Like, let's just put it out there. I own that, and I have the right to own that. People will even go as far to correct me: 'Oh no, you're curvy, you're voluptuous.' Listen, I'm fat! I make no qualms about it. I'm not here to argue about it. I'm not here to defend it. It is who I am. It is an identifier that I have chosen. That I'm very comfortable with. So that's me."

Short and sweet, this is US. We are visible and unashamed. We are who we are. We make no qualms about it.

WHEN WORKING OUT WAS HARDLY WORKING AND ONE COULD NOT EAT ANY LESS

If I Hear "Calories in, Calories out" One More Time!

It was the summer of 2011. I had just hiked up a hill for the first time in I don't know how long. I had started a new job, and the hill was part of my hiring package. My body was struggling. I was out of breath and feeling defeated. I thought to myself how much better life would be in the event I dropped a few pounds. As I rode on the PRT (West Virginia University's little train system for transportation across campus), I thought about the changes I could implement. By the time I got my next check, I knew what exercise plan I was going to undertake. I contacted my older sister and asked for my "fanny lifter" back. The fanny lifter was a two-tier step used in The Firm™ workout tapes. I traveled to Pennsylvania over a weekend to get it. I returned home and set everything up. I also remembered from horrors past that working out would *never* be enough if I wanted to see results (the workout videos also do a good job at reminding you of this), so I had to devise a revised eating plan or as I like to call it, a DIET.

To refute the rubbish, I grew up living in my body set to disprove stereotypes. I *danced*. And not that two-step you think of at the family cookout. No. I danced choreography for years. As a kid, I learned the Janet Jackson videos. Who could see me when Hammer was on the TV?! I learned how to pop after watching *Breakin'*. I was the largest member of the dance team at my church for ten years. I refused to let my weight disqualify me for things I knew my body was capable of. I refused to let someone else tell me what my body couldn't do. Every time my A1c tests (for diabetes) came back, I'd watch doctors look puzzled or disheartened. When I had to snap back at family members to assert that I did not in fact have diabetes, silence would fill the room. To walk in confidence in this body, draped in fabric that clung to my shape or showed my thighs, was a rebellious act. So rebellious I was, but not without first being scathed.

I started counting calories at about the 1,800 mark and made a goal to work out three to four times a week. Sorrowful now, I celebrated the days when I ate less and still remained on my feet. Soon 1,800 turned into 1,500. My workout regimen increased to five days a week. My body started to shrink. So did my trust in the ability to oversee my food intake. As with most disordered eating patterns (Center for Discovery, n.d.), I thought about food most of the day. If it wasn't about eating, it was about prepping, or not eating. My workouts also took over my days and thoughts. I often wondered how I would still be active while I was away visiting family. Two rest days in a week?!? Not an option! I carried my weights and alternative foods in my trunk to travel when I would be away from home more than two days. I'm a Capricorn. If you know us, you know we plan so we never have to speak of failure.

I was attracted to the weight or pant-size goals. I wanted to be smaller because I felt it would enable me to do more. I wanted to be stronger. I didn't want to struggle to make it up another hill. I never thought to myself that if I just practiced at climbing the hill, I would get better. I had internalized a certain belief about fat bodies. We were incapable of doing the least. It also never occurred to me that people in smaller bodies also had to practice climbing hills to be good at it.

What's even more telling was that I was only at that job for about four months. In four months, the hill was gone, but I was left with this "fight" I started within myself. This was because I had already internalized messages around what larger bodies did not have the capabilities to do. I was set to roll down a hill on fire with no brakes. I wish I would've had the inspiration I do today from fat Black badasses like Amanda Gilliam of Big Girl Barbell, who has been powerlifting for ages in a larger body! I wish I would've known fat Black advocates like Courtney Marshall, who works tirelessly to ensure people have access to body movement plans that accommodate their bodies. But I didn't, and it over time began to show.

As my body got smaller, people noticed. High fives, smiles, catcalls, you name it. My muscles began to show through my skin. It was as though I had become a better person overnight! This new reality I walked into was one that appeared to be better than the reality I lived in riding home on that PRT. It was like the scene when Dorothy and them in *The Wiz* stroll up to Emerald City for the first time. Awe filled my heart as I watched people pay me more attention than I had seen every day for the past two years. Interesting how I was bigger before but invisible. Scary that the only thing I needed was to be thin(ner) to be seen as worthy to lead, be seen with, or be acknowledged (Stryker 2016).

It wasn't too long before the dizzy spells started. I had to stand up slow to avoid the room spinning. Knowing that this symptom would pass, I would wait to start my day. My body also was starting to feel a little sorer than usual. No worries. I would just keep pushing on. I had a schedule and read a Google article that said something like you start to lose the muscle you build after two days if you don't keep working on it. I was jumping over towels, sumo squatting, and burpeeing my way to "fitness." I found out what food I could have at KFC and felt great knowing I could still eat fast food, albeit the chicken was rotisserie. Can you believe I was stopping at Wendy's and asking for a salad? Whew! The salad was trash and I was just happy to know it was a side, so I did not have to pay extra for it. I was down a few more pounds, and if these were the little hiccups I needed to endure, so be it.

The idea of drinking regular soda terrified me. The calories that I needed to count for the amount of soda I consumed were just not doable under my plan. I substituted this with diet soda. I traded sugar for artificial sweeteners. Hamburger for turkey (one of the saddest days of my life). The pain in my body hadn't let up. Neither did the dizziness. All this work I had been doing accounted for a total of roughly 40 pounds. I never made it under 250 pounds.

The public didn't know that though. I remember telling my sister this during a conversation, and she seemed startled.

People kept going on about how different I looked and how much weight I had lost. If they only knew that eating between 1,200 and 1,500 calories a day and working out five days a week with cardio and strength-training combined resulted in a loss of only 40 pounds over three years, they'd be shocked. I was. I remember questioning why the scale wasn't moving. I knew I couldn't afford to eat any less. I also knew there were only two other days in the week when I was not working out, and my body was already in pain. Where was all the "calories in, calories out" help now?! The ability to keep the 40 pounds I'd lost at bay took the same, if not more, energy. I became overly critical of my body. Obsessive over my diet.

Living alone provides you with a type of liberty that is unprecedented. Wanna wear clothes? No. Walk around naked. Want to eat ice cream for dinner? Sure. Who's gonna stop you? A downside to this though is that no one can really stop you. Living alone provided me with the space I needed to run my "fitness factory." I filled my fridge and cupboards with only the foods I thought would fuel my body into progress. I crafted out a space in my living room and bedroom for working out so I didn't get discouraged prior to, from moving things. I had enough space that I would jump rope indoors! Every body movement I could think of, I made room for. Every time I was able to do something different with my body, I accredited it to my regimen. Every time I was not hassled during flights because of seating, I was grateful for my regimen. Healthism had become my life. I was drowning and didn't even know it.

The idea that good things proceed from the steps you take toward health is rooted in ableism. The saying that you cannot love someone else until you love yourself follows this line of thinking. As humans, we do not need to do to be found worthy. Our bodies are more than machines working toward the next best thing. Sometimes, the next best thing is in us, being still and accepting. Not wrestling, attempting to change or modify—just resting. Healthism does not allow for this. Healthism argues that you receive good because you do good by your body. I clap back and say, no, society rewards those who they *think* do good by their bodies.

I'll never forget the number of times people have told me, "You're not that big." I'll never forget the incompetence most of us have in knowing how much a person weighs by simply looking at them. I think if we'd be honest, we'd admit that our expertise in sizing is elementary at best. We cannot tell what 400 pounds looks like. We would not know 153 pounds if it walked past us and sat on our laps! And if we'd be honest about this, we'd also have to be honest about "health." What can we tell about a person's health from looking at them? Are they sick or are they just having a bad day? Is it cancer or the common cold? I worked out and monitored my food intake religiously for two-plus years and was still considered fat . . . overweight . . . AND obese! By the standards of society, I was doing more than most and still considered unhealthy. Without a body to match the effort I was putting in, I came to realize that I would never be accepted as "healthy." No, I'd be in the "Well, at least you're trying to do something about it" group. Maybe even the "Wow! You look great" group. But the group that we typically seek to be a member of—the one that stops the chuckles when we go to the gym or is amazed that we can run up a flight of stairs and not be out of breath—will forever elude fat bodies.

It was a heartbreaking reality I had to see for myself. I had to sit myself down and ask how long I wanted to keep being friends with something that had no intention on friending me back. Memories of mornings and evenings flooded my mind that encompassed clothes I tucked away in my closet to wear once I was 15 or 20 pounds lighter. Them clothes cost me good money! Was I now just supposed to give them up? I searched for reasons other than the ones rooted in diet culture to hold on to my original goals. I was saving money after all, and doing my part in lessening my footprint by not tossing the outfits. I was helping the earth, yes? No.

I'd like to say that breaking free from healthism was this joyous, celebratory event that was followed by me opting out of being active and eating everything that healthism swears I should not eat until my heart was content, but it wasn't. Instead, it was staring in the mirror until the rolls on my body looked normal. It was standing, staring in the mirror until I could normalize those stretch marks that ran across my belly with no sense of direction. It was tough. In this space, I was being confronted with all the messages I had heard over the past thirty years. Feelings of never being good enough, pretty enough, or slim enough filled my head.

Good enough for what, you ask? EVERYTHING! How would I get married and have children with a body no one wanted? How would I travel the world with a body that cost twice as much to fit in airplane seats? (I have never had to pay for two seats, by the way.) What would my headshots look like on the campus website? The cheeks on my face were already large. Was I ready for them to grow even more?! What was one to do with this full-figured melanated body that, even if it was smaller, would still be considered unattractive and unqualified?

By all accounts, healthism had duped me into believing that the effort alone of trying to be smaller was worth some benefit even if I'd never make it there! It whispered for me to try again, even though I was well aware that trying hadn't gotten me far. By 2014, in many ways, it actually had cycled me backward. The weight was coming back . . . quickly. I had been working long days and nights toward my master's degree. I had to switch up my routine. Five days of working out turned into four. My diet remained pretty much intact. I had a choice to make again that had haunted me from years before. Play a part in my own cycle of insanity or do something different.

It's no wonder the weight loss industry is worth $72 billion (*BusinessWire* 2019)! We are left striving for the unrealistic, investing in teas, lollipops, gym equipment, and the like to conform our bodies into something they will never be. And it's hard to give up that fantasy. The fantasy plays on TVs and Instagram feeds across the nation. We are constantly doused with the rhetoric of healthism, despite it being illogical. Health, in and of itself, is subjective (Sadistic 2019). The idea that bodies, our bodies, should all be the same size despite our height, or genetics, or choice is foolish. To think that I or anyone else owes society a body that is a size drafted from a body that was never our own is grossly unrealistic. We are now at a point in society where even research states it is natural for women to dislike their bodies (Runfola et al. 2013). But why?

What is it about a fat body that is so offensive? How on earth does the melanin in my skin incite a frown? Have you *seen* this skin in the sun?! Whew! The golden undertones that highlight my cheekbones are glorious! The rolls that make up my person are warm and inviting. No one that has been embraced by them leaves unsatisfied. In my hands, there is healing. In my presence, I house joy.

Undertaking intuitive eating (a term I wouldn't learn until later) was a struggle. Though not uncommon, listening to your body cues to know when or what to eat is altered in society, as we are generally taught we need at least three meals a day with foods that are included in the "food pyramid" (Association for Size Diversity and Health, n.d.). Aside from the fact that this pyramid is extremely Eurocentric and doesn't adequately incorporate diverse variations of foods and meals, the three meals a day rule becomes even more complicated when dieting is introduced (Melton 2018). Three meals can easily turn into six smaller meals, or be a fast, or only include certain foods that probably go against what our body is seeking after. We are indoctrinated at a very early age to distrust what our body tells us. We are taught that cravings are undesirable and abnormal compared to what the body needs. In this context, the body is our enemy, and we have been tasked to master it.

Looking back, I'm grateful I was able to recover. While I was never diagnosed with an eating disorder, roughly 13 percent of Black women suffer from one (J. Y. Taylor et al. 2007). Due to the bias in treatment for Black women, victims typically go unnoticed (Beebe 2018). Moreover, if you are fat and Black, you're more likely to be turned away for treatment or simply not believed (Khakh 2019).

I'd watch the clock and wonder how I could be hungry again after just three hours? I consciously had to make decisions not to read caloric information on the backs of all the food I consumed. My body, ravaged from disordered eating, did not house within itself the trust to determine what I could eat and when. Craving sweets was a "problem" I had to work to embrace. I had to unlearn the cycle of "eat this, not that." I had to allow my body to trust again.

5

ACCEPTANCE +
RESISTANCE = ACTIVISM

The tug-of-war fat people are cast into can have us swinging at anything that moves! Being thrown into a fight due to accepting ourselves can cause our guards to be up most of the time. A way I found to balance the pressure of always having something thrown at me was to muster up a piece of courage to throw something back. When I realized folks really didn't want no smoke and were hoping I'd drop my head in shame, I knew I had found a strength in my person. I had found a piece of my voice that folks didn't think I had. Now, I haven't always been good at math, but if I were to create an equation based off my own lived experience, I'd argue that acceptance (i.e., embracing of oneself) plus resistance (i.e., the ability to fight back) equals activism (i.e., smoke). And this ain't no "not sure of myself, I think that's what the literature says" smoke. Nah, this is that "I got time today, you really thought that joke you told was funny, or that listing your credentials before you spewed a bunch of racist fatphobic hyperbole was

go'n get you off the hook," smoke. Folks don't want none of
that. When I was able to identify the majority of the pressure I
received from others as a form of bullying, fighting back became
easier and easier. At one point, I was fighting because I was
looking for smoke, and I had to stop myself to assess if fighting
some battles were worth it at all. Smoke is cool sometimes, but
even the smoke you can handle has a way of wearing at your
well-being. Nevertheless, my strength was there. I also found
that with the strength I was obtaining, I had the capacity to
strengthen others.

Given the gaslighting that comes with being fat in this
country, we often can see where bias and discrimination are
taking place while others question our judgment. Responses
like "They didn't really mean it in that way" or "Are you sure
you're not reading too much into things?" are common statements heard around the globe related to fatphobia. If you add
being Black into the picture, many of us get accused of fighting
about *everything* and carrying our politics on our sleeves. One
can only imagine the hell we catch for refusing to allow people
to treat or talk to us any kind of way. Those who defend or
explain bias as being implicit, without holding parties account-
able, only weaken the fight for liberation, as what is not readily
seen by the offender is often always seen by those they offend.
Folks' attempts at telling us that someone didn't really mean
to offend us, or that they weren't fully aware of the harm they
were causing, fall upon deaf ears. Especially in today's climate.
As a minority, Black people are inundated with information
about the majority. We are not given a choice to turn off the
constant ringing in our ears that is White America. We have to
learn about their version of history, their version of living, and
even their version of culture, despite being in it. Ain't that some
shit?! I'm in the story but can't even tell it! I'm in the story
but "Bill" (we all know the "Bills" who live nothing but know

everything) and all his comrades are steadily telling me that what I know I experienced was wrong and inaccurate. We need activism for this reason. We need folks who will be interrupters and upheave the damage that has been done, turning over the narratives of our lived experiences back into our hands. We have never been okay with being spoken over or silenced. We are far past the space of having dialogues if actionable change is not on the itinerary. Why should we afford others the luxury of learning from us without compensation for our labor and time, considering learning about them was a requirement that held and still holds grave consequences if we misstep? Activism doesn't have to be rude, but it also doesn't have to give out discounts and extensions on learning the lessons necessary for our survival.

So much of what is happening in activism as it relates to fat bodies actually happens online (Cox 2018). That isn't to say that there aren't bodies "on the ground" risking being paraded online as a meme or even risking their livelihood to stand up for the rights of those in larger bodies. Some do participate in protests and other forms of collective action to get the message of fat acceptance across. For example, between 2017 and the present day, disability rights activists have partnered with fat activists to protest health care changes and the implementation of including fat or "obesity" as a "pre-existing condition" (*Democracy Now!* 2017). Interpersonally, other fat activists advocate for their rights at doctors' offices, refusing to be weighed or requesting that doctors give them weight-neutral solutions to their health ailments (Sterry and Sturtevant 2015). Still, there are many different outlets that allow fat activists an opportunity to voice themselves uncompromisingly in their own way via blogs, social media, and other online avenues. Some activists have found a way to merge their passion for liberation with business, creating fashionwear and accessories for the modern fat Black womxn.

Entrepreneurs like Rita Jane come to mind, as Malaika Apparel
is a fashion line curated for those who are passionate about the
nuances of Black culture and wearing clothing with a statement.
Brands like Fat Mermaids and Carefree Fat Girl create clothing
specifically for fat people and provide a heavy dose of snark to
diet culture and its supporters. Finding acceptance is the gate-
way to open up waves of creativity that liberate the mind and
heart to find a lane that works for the individual. When you are
liberated, it is less about what's on trend and more about what
works for you. For me, I found my ability to fight in speaking,
researching, and writing.

Being part of academia, I am well aware of the barriers that
exist for Black scholars—from researching topics that are seen
as taboo to getting tenure. The looks on the faces of those when
I tell them what I study are of confusion and, sometimes, regret.
I've been told not to be the Black scholar who only researches
"Black" things. One could only imagine that this rule also
applies to being the fat scholar who only researches fat things.
Guess I failed at avoiding both topics immensely. I also realized
that earlier on, academia would not be the best fit for me. Seeing
the barriers clear before me, and having to deal with fatphobia
from colleagues in their discussions of my topic of choice, let me
know that if I was going to really aim toward creating change,
it would need to be done outside of the ivory towers. I knew my
departure was sure, but not before I did work that solidified my
mark in the field. While present, I knew that I stood in a position
that afforded me a certain amount of privilege that could be
used to create change.

Choosing to study identity within the context of larger
bodies was not an easy choice, but I was determined to find
a way to say something different about this body I have the
honor of living in. I wanted to ensure that the next generation
of individuals passing through these topics would be able to

scroll through the artifacts of the past and find that someone, somewhere, decided to stand up and speak against the cruelty directed toward fat bodies. I wanted this shit documented! And not just documented anywhere. No, I wanted people to look through some of the most prestigious places in our society (like the grand ol' ivory towers) and find that someone raised their voice to say that society was wrong for how they had treated fat bodies, and that the struggle experienced by those living in fat Black bodies was different from that of the White experience. If resistance was something that I would have to deal with whether I wanted it or not, then I would choose to resist in my own way, on my own terms.

In 2013, I had finished up my first year in my master's program and made a decision that would ultimately change my path as a scholar. I embarked on a journey into the world of fat acceptance like a bat out of hell. I told my advisor in my master's program that I wanted to change what I studied. I signed up for classes that I barely grasped, in hopes of understanding identity and stigma. My methodology of assessment became qualitative. I was leading participant observation studies at local gyms to see how fatphobic class instructors were. Though this was a preliminary study, it was wonderful to see what so many articles now point out. Weight stigma (i.e., fatphobic remarks) changed the environment of those being active in it. Morale would drop when fatphobic language was present. Morale would increase when more inclusive language around working hard or achieving goals was used. In one of my first actions of activism in this arena, I submitted my report to the facility that gave me permission to do the observations. They were grateful for the feedback, although I cannot speak to if changes were made. Being present in the study did help me to dispel stereotypes of what it means to live in a larger body and move it. Dance classes were roughly an hour long, with a strength-training component at the end. I stayed for it all. I also then went somewhere secluded to write down my observation notes. It was a beautiful bouquet of controlled chaos.

My master's thesis examined the perceptions of individuals when they were exposed to pictures of fat people with and without heads. I still remember, to this day, a thesis committee member encouraging the idea that this topic could, in fact, become a book. Who knew?! I didn't!

To successfully defend my thesis on this platform was a sign not only that I was on the right track, but that examining this phenomenon provided valuable insight into the society we live in. I was not just a person sailing (more like climbing in rugged terrain) through academia in hopes of obtaining a degree. I was someone who wanted to leverage what she studied to change the world. For me, fatphobia and weight stigma were a silent killer of sorts wreaking havoc on communities near and far. It was a soul-crushing epidemic. Very few have escaped its grasp unscathed. Slightly in disbelief, I successfully defended my thesis and received my degree. My thesis was in writing. I had accomplished my goal. In the span of two to three years, I would go on and present roughly twice an academic year on the topic of weight stigma. I was making headway *even* with the side-eyes and looks of regret. Those things began to matter less. The mission began to matter more.

I would receive full funding to pursue my PhD on weight stigma and identity in 2014. I once again packed my bags and my car and traveled to another part of the United States to continue the journey in being loud on behalf of fat acceptance. New people gave new looks. I remained unbothered. With four years to complete my PhD, I did so in three years and eight months. With people questioning the validity of the work that we as fat activists do, I obtained a whole PhD degree studying the Fat Liberation Movement. But that wasn't enough. I knew I wanted to transition out of academia and be more involved in community. The heart of my work was with people, not accolades. I needed the community to know that what I do, I do for us. The skill set I learned in obtaining my degrees was just another tool to add to our ability to change the narrative.

Launching the podcast *Fresh Out the Cocoon* was a way to expand my reach and give my fingers a break, as writing can be exhausting. Through much of my studies, I always noticed how the voices of those most marginalized were muted. I wanted to include voices in the community besides myself. I wanted to create a platform where my sisters in the LGBTQ+ community could speak for themselves. I wanted to hear from my family throughout the diaspora on their lived experiences. I knew that though my voice had relevance, so did theirs. By now, I was saying it loud: "I'm Black and I'm proud . . . and fat!" I was shouting, "Black fat Lives Matter too!" I was thirsty for a community and family. I knew I couldn't be the only one. Matter of fact, I was pretty sure I was late to this party.

Black folk have always had subsets and groups of resistance to tackle the inequalities that were unique to their own struggles (K. Taylor 2016). Their choice to fight while accepting their identities is well documented in history: throughout the civil rights movement, the maintenance of the Black Panther Party, the fight for women's rights, the #MeToo movement, and Black Lives Matter, just to name a few. Additionally, there is no end to those who have been fighting on the ground, never seeking recognition, while serving their community. Daily, calls for support from fat Black women to advocate for the needs of others fill my social media timelines to stop evictions, pay past-due bills, provide an out for domestic violence victims, and assist in supplying needs like coats and food. They do this all by centering Black voices and experiences without the commentary of White folk.

In these spaces, acceptance and resistance meld wonderfully to energize the magic in us. Surely, society has awakened the wrong Black girls, who have lived long enough to know how to navigate around institutional barriers to supply their communities with the things they are in desperate need of. Society caught us on a day when we had time, y'all. They caught us when we were fed up with living an invisible life while being hypervisible. There is not enough black fabric in the world that could hide the stature in which we stand. Even if they could not see us, indeed our voices are being heard.

Often I hear people talk about the "real" fight and how it ought to be fought. For me, if this notion is not carefully examined, we will only perpetuate the same cliquish tendencies, ousting those who do things differently from us because we do not agree. It is factual that armies have always fought with the best strategy that has worked for them as a group. Not everyone can or will gather for protests, nor should they. Not everyone can call their local senator or representative to demand something be changed. Activism is about raising awareness for change, and participating to make change a reality. If someone's activism doesn't cause harm to the collective, then the collective should chill out. We can't be wasting all of our good smoke for one another, y'all!

The generation rising in the footsteps of their ancestors are not interested in being "good fatties" by societal standards, doing whatever we can to seem as though we are working toward a smaller body (Stryker 2016). We are not interested in hedging statements about what we ate with remarks on working out or restricting consumption later. We are not afraid to wear colors. The bright kind. The way yellow complements all shades of the chocolate spectrum is more than enough reason to keep adorning ourselves in it.

Additionally, we have shunned being the other type of "good fatty" in White-dominated spaces that comes to the rescue of White folks who do not know how to hold their tongues when overstepping boundaries related to the fat Black experience. No, we are not interested in coddling White fears in hopes of being accepted later. We want our table and chairs, and we want them now. We also are not asking. By the time this book is read, we will be well off in the process of building our own.

BEING ON THE GROUND
DOING THIS WORK

Being involved in activism, though often romanticized in the mainstream, is no easy task. People have dedicated their lives to organizing and coordinating work that is both effective and equitable. Utilizing some of my own resources, I've managed to do research in a way that has compensated participants for their time and elevated their voices authentically.

Being thrown into a fight is never easy. It takes a bit of adjusting to catch your groove. Many of my guests on *Fresh Out the Cocoon* were involved in activist work, finding their own lanes and creating something that challenged the status quo of what is defined as "normal." One of these trailblazers, Tiana Dodson, found her lane as a fitness trainer starting a program overseas in Germany to change the narrative about fat bodies. She detailed her journey and the creation of her training program, The One Beautiful YES!, that inspires participants to start saying "yes" to life, rejecting the "nos" so often heard from others due to their body size. I sat down to talk with Tiana and discuss what it was like trying to fit into spaces that really didn't serve her purpose, and constantly butting heads with doctors who demanded she lose weight despite her blood work coming back normal: "Through my training, eventually I got okay with it [being fat], and I stood up and said, 'Yes, I'm fat!' . . . I discovered Health at Every Size and that was like, ta da! Everything was just perfect!"

Adrienne Ray, owner of the plus-size consignment shop Curve Conscious, also talked about how she wanted to translate her interests in clothing and the environment into activism efforts for the underserved fat population. During her visit to the podcast, she was clear that she had found a niche market in consignment that could fulfill her passion for helping others and fulfill a need for larger bodies: "It really came down to: *Dammmmn*, a girl is fat and can't find fresh thrifted clothes! That's what it came down to. I realized I wasn't the only person who struggled in a larger body to find fresh thrifted clothes. So, this was something that would not only be a positive, plus for me and my life but I'm sure several others. I definitely wanted my business to help others and fulfill a need and fill a void."

Lastly, counselor Lenese Stephens talked about how her activism work was spurred by her own tumultuous relationship with her body and therapy. Using her research in academia as a conduit, she carved out a space for her practice, Hopeful Counseling, and attracts many fat Black clients as a result: "When I did my bio, I made sure to put in my bio 'My research is geared toward the plus-size community,' and in essence of highlighting the quality of life for African American plus-size women. So knowing that that is in my bio and people can read that, I do have a large population of clients I serve that are plus-size women, and they are definitely seeking the therapy and mental health services of how to become more empowered."

When we are liberated, it makes room for us to flourish in creativity and help someone else get free. It is fascinating to see the ideas of others come to life while providing a service that replicates the process.

BULLSHIT MEASURES:
TOSS THE TAPE AND THE BMI

I held the tip of the tightly coiled measuring tape and watched it unravel. Sixty inches. Sixty inches was the length of the tape from start to finish. Though I was excited to be making my own clothes, I wasn't thrilled about being measured. Being measured was very much like standing on the scale. The numbers just keep going up without your permission, and what's worse than that nurse with her crusty finger sliding the weight little by little until she has your weight down to the ounce! I was not interested in that type of monitoring. Nonetheless, if I wanted to make something that fit me, I needed to measure how much fabric I would need.

I threw the tape out as far as I could, holding on to one end. I needed to have a good idea of how much tape I had to use to measure the circumference of my flesh. I held on tightly to the end of the tape, pressing it into my belly button. Taking the rest of the tape, I stretched, then wrapped the rest of the tape around my waist to meet me in the middle. "Thirty-six and a half," I said. Granted, the tape was a bit snug, but there was no way I was giving up that half an inch! What value was in a half an inch? Looking back, I really can't say; but at the time, I thought a whole lot. The idea of measurement would often get under my skin. Measuring my hips was the worst! I remember the moment when the tape ran out and I had to guess the number. I felt left out . . . so big I could not be measured.

In my own research, much grief has come from the body mass index (BMI), a tool created by a statistician with an interest in human growth but no real understanding of how bodies work (Cox 2018). Participants in interviews often lamented that the BMI was weaponized against them, despite all their other markers of "health" being in good standing. The BMI's relevancy has been long debated, but these uproars have mostly fallen on deaf ears because of *who* is raising the issue (Bacon and Severson 2019). It is common for people in smaller bodies to contend that fat folk should just lose the weight. They make it seem like it is as easy as sliding on a slick patch of ice you didn't see. I mean, if it were really that easy, it would work for most, right? Except it doesn't. Matta fact (read as "matter of fact"), it doesn't work for pretty much 95 percent of us who try (Gaesser 2009). So how does something that only seems to be fairly successful for 5 percent of those who try get recommended to the 100 percent as though it is wildly successful? The BMI is a good place to start.

When the National Institutes of Health changed the definitions around who qualified to be overweight in 1998 (Nuttall 2015), eyebrows were raised as to the meaning of fat and how bodies were measured. Could your health simply be determined by your weight and height? Seemingly overnight, individuals who were considered "normal" weight went to sleep and woke up "overweight." Moreover, the BMI has a racist past, as much adopted by the West does.

When I attended college in 2008 (I was a late bloomer), I remember being astonished and disheartened by the "research" done to represent Black people. In every category, we were most likely to be sick and die. We were the least educated. We were the least "fit." I wondered . . . pondered where these researchers were finding all these sick, destitute Black folks! After all, the Black people I grew up around often loved life and lived well into old age. The prevalence of sickness and disease was such a big topic in my classes and was spoken about like the plague. Like, if you were Black, you'd be bound to die of some type of cancer. Oh, and diabetes. We all get that.

It's not surprising that there was a study conducted that argued the BMI overestimates both fatness and sickness in the Black community. In fact, it would be on par with what has already been discussed thus far in this book, as it relates to racism and healthism. The assumption that Black folks eat more because they have larger bodies is fatphobic. The assumption that Black folk are larger in general is also fatphobic. This impacts someone like me, who could be described as "healthy" based on blood work and other markers, because I must deal with the bullshit baggage of the BMI that some physicians are unwilling to unpack (Nuttall 2015). They're unwilling to unpack their assumptions about me and those that look like me. They're unwilling to confront the lies they have been taught in the books by which they have obtained their degree. So, I am left to hear all the lectures on healthy choices and small changes that ultimately will bring me to this land of milk (almond of course) and honey overflowing with kale, scales, and pro tein shakes.

The treatment that fat bodies endure in examination rooms across the country is daunting. The labor exerted by those who live in fat bodies along with the intersections of other identities is exhausting. I know, because I live this. Friendly bigoted doctors smile in my face, experts in communication, and attempt to reframe weight loss because *they* cannot come to grips that a fat Black girl is comfortable in her own skin. They look at me, tell me my numbers are good and I have nothing to worry about; however, I could have something to worry about in the future based on their idea that fat causes sickness. I say this last point because their argument has no basis, looking at my numbers. What they are referring to are the studies that exaggerate Black fatness and sickness.

What patient wants to hear news that they are fine today but may be in danger of dying tomorrow based on unfounded evidence that relates to them personally? Apparently, Black fat folks. And to dispute this is to be non-compliant. To be noncompliant is to stir up the wrath of a physician already on the verge of despising your existence, because they do not think you care enough about your own body to make prescribed changes (Phelan et al. 2015). It is a never-ending cycle and struggle of power dynamics between the voiced and the voiceless.

Most recently, I came across a clothing brand that has been a godsend! eShakti is a brand offering clothes up to a size 36W. They will even customize your clothes by request for a small upcharge of 12 percent of the garment's list price. The catch? You have to measure yourself.

As I prepared to travel to Jamaica for a friend's wedding, I had a dress custom-made by eShakti. It fits me like a glove. I had to measure myself to get it. I had to wrap that tape measure around these hips and estimate inches when the tape measure ran out. I measured my arms and beautifully stretched waist as well. My discomfort with being measured revisited me during this process, but I was not the same little fat Black girl I was so many years ago. This fat Black girl has now found a place in the world *even* if it does not find "home" in her. Through her hard-fought battle with healthism, she has come out of the ruins, with her own definition of health birthed out of necessity and survival in a society that does not see her existence as a priority.

I planned to dance in the dress I ordered, knowing it was crafted for me. This was not my wedding, but I was celebrating new beginnings. I had no intentions of letting scales, which I had literally outgrown some years ago, to any degree determine my worth. Time to ditch the measures that will never measure up! Time to define this thing called acceptance for ourselves!

Part 3

My Community, My People

6

IT'S A FAMILY REUNION!

hat is it like to come upon a scene where there are NOTH-
ING but folks that look like you, have been through
what you are going through, and stand ready to encourage? I've never been to heaven, but I'm sure the feeling is close.
Black fat spaces have been lifesavers, literally, for many. And I'm
not talking about spaces where your size 14's and 16's get to talk
about their "plus-size" struggles in wanting a piece of clothing
in an XL but couldn't find it *anywhere*. No, I'm speaking of
the spaces that center super- and "infini" fats, who do not have
resources (from clothes to materials that assist them in hygiene)
readily accessible to them in brick-and-mortar stores. These are
the sizes of individuals the general public is referring to when
they speak about knowing someone is unhealthy by simply looking at them. They are in these spaces, living life unapologetically,
finding healing, and passing on encouragement to others.

Stumbling upon these meeting places was almost surreal.
I took a chance when hearing about different groups through
online networks of fat advocacy, also known as the "Fatosphere," and began to explore. In my mind, I didn't have much

to lose as it related to finding more people like myself. After all, I was in a location that didn't provide much for adult entertainment in general, so finding a niche like Black fat adult entertainment was pretty much unheard of. I'm also an introvert and could not have guaranteed that I'd want to be out and about with people whom I didn't know. Being able to access community online had hit a sweet spot for me, and if that was a space full of fat Black women, even better! I had spent so much time in online spaces that spoke about inclusion yet were filled primarily with White folk. The same old repetitive explanations filled my timelines about privilege, allyship, and safe spaces, but no *real* work was being fostered among members. At the same speed that a post could go up about fatphobia, a comment dismissive of the realities experienced by more marginalized members would also present itself, challenging me to make a decision. Community or peace? I needed to find a community where I did not have to choose. I wanted to live in the freedom of ALL my identities and not just the ones that were palatable in the mainstream. Luckily, I was not alone. When I entered these groups, the experiences of others were so similar, it was like hearing myself talk. So many had ventured into these spaces looking for inclusivity. So many had journeyed from other groups that lacked awareness of biases and privilege as related to social conditions and resources. We could talk to each other about where to find proper undergarments for clothes AND the struggle of being Black and fat. There was no need to sugarcoat that our race played a role in how we were perceived by others.

One online group stands out among the rest when I think of the liberation of fat Black girls, women, and femmes. Magical Fat Black Girls was originally founded in 2015 by Brandi Wharton, who later modified the name to Magical Fat Black Femmes (MFBF) in 2017. An OG of Facebook groups, MFBF has been one of the longest-standing BLACK body-positive, fat-affirming

spaces I've ever been a member of. No code-switching necessary. Moreover, in this space, real change happens. So many
of the members there have gone on to do great things in their
communities and through online networks. Through MFBF, an
inclusionary Black extension of the Fatosphere has been created. Need to know where to shop? We got you. Need to know
the best sites for dating while fat? We got you. Need to know
resources for navigating towns, cities, and states being fat? We
got you. Black and queer? We. Got. You. Rolling up in this space,
it felt like how all the family reunions in the past should've felt.
I heard "yasssss" and "ayyyyeeee" when I posted me dressed in
something nice. We shared videos of us dancing, cheering each
other on in support.

We also got serious about the trauma and ignorance many
of us were raised in. We unpacked internalized stigma around
our body image and simple tasks that most don't think twice
about in public (i.e., grocery shopping, eating out, going to
the gym, etc.). We addressed the importance of mental health
and seeking therapy with the resources passed throughout the
group. We stood watch for our sisters who felt suicidal, checking on them and sending members near them on foot when
we could. We upheld and affirmed the trans experience. We
learned what not to say and do in love. This learning experience wasn't like the ones I encountered in predominantly White
spaces. There was a sincerity in seeking and learning. There
was also less skepticism around the topic being taught by those
who lent their labor. We were open and honest without judgment. MFBF was the reality we had needed for our younger
selves. It was the life-giving source for those whom the world
turned its back on ages ago.

MFBF was one of the inspirations for deciding to be more
vocal about my stance on fat acceptance and the Black experience. It became all the more real by being in the group that my

experience was just a piece of the puzzle. I could not, nor did I desire to, speak for *all* fat Black women. I did, however, want these stories to be heard. I wanted everyone in our community to experience the liberation I was experiencing. I started to brainstorm about ways that I could make this happen. My podcast was on the horizon, and I didn't even know it yet. My journey to find family one by one continued.

Crystal Newman was one of the first fat Black activists I met on my "reunion circuit" back in 2016–17. At the time, I was preparing to travel cross-country to attend the Popular Culture Association (PCA) academic conference. I had heard about Crystal's work previously with Fat Positive Louisville (Dickman 2017), a fat-activism group she helped create on the campus of the University of Louisville, and looked forward to meeting them. Newman, a suicide survivor and a fierce advocate of intersectional awareness, spoke on a panel about activism and the nuances of the fat Black experience through the lens of someone who is also Black and queer. I was interested in their take on things. I was also surprised that this type of activism was happening in a place like Kentucky! We exchanged contact information and have remained connected since. I had located a sister. I was on my way to reconnecting with the rest of the family.

I also created T-shirt designs on the *Fresh Out the Cocoon* website that reflected how I perceived that the fat community might want to be represented. My T-shirts had all types of sayings for those that were loud and proud (i.e., Fat and Dope as Fuck!) and those who wanted to say something without "shouting" (i.e., These Curves Tho). During that time, I found myself in conversation regularly with one of the powerhouses in fat forward fashion, Jai Mobley of Fat Mermaids. Jai was pretty and soft-spoken. Her smile was bright, and you could just tell that all the pink she used in her designs was a reflection of the light that shone inwardly.

The conversations we shared about business were open and honest. I got the feeling that we both wanted to see each other win. When she would be mentioned in the media, I would share the news. When I was mentioned, she'd do the same. We were sisters helping one another strive to reach our goals in our own way. She also connected me with one of the best body-positive illustrators in the game!

Marlena Jones of Marlena Jones Illustration started to assist me in bringing my ideas to life. She drew fat bodies like they looked! Y'all, she was drawing me, and my aunties, and my grams, and I was grateful. Different shades, different shapes, and all realistic. Her talent was unmatched. Her conviction was very similar to that of Jai's and me. Working with her felt more like when you get together with friends, laugh, joke, and then get work done. It felt like being among family. Jai, Marlena, and I all shared with each other. We were practicing community just like I remember it from growing up in the projects. Reunion was in full swing, even if it was happening in spurts and individually.

This cycle would repeat itself several times over, and would continue even after the launch of the podcast. I met the good sis Rita Bunatal, founder of Malaika Apparel, through our membership in some of the same groups. Rita's focus has been on creating fashion draped in the essence of Black culture, fusing African American and Ghanaian influences. Our mission to change the world through awareness aligned.

Erica Ware stepped into my life randomly during the time when I lost my father, and she offered support regularly. We did not know each other, but she stepped in out of compassion. Her commitment to changing how folks see fat girls by working specifically with fat girls has been an encouragement in knowing we are passing something valuable on to the next generation.

The reciprocal support. The celebration of wins. The reassurance in doubt. These are all the qualities my reunion led me to.

Family by mission and vision. Blood did not have to be a factor. We are connected through the DNA of lived experiences.

Even as I type, I can hear "Never Knew Love Like This Before" by Stephanie Mills playing in my head! It's true too! We are sisters in service. We are family.

Through the implementation of the podcast, I have been able to interview some of the most profound women with stories that inspire and relate to others living in fat Black bodies. Through analyzing episodes, I've found common themes that most of my interviewees speak about, and I feel that is an inspiration for why they are committed to the work they do. Between 2016 and 2019, I have had the privilege to record twenty-two episodes, with twelve of those featuring a guest. Each episode lasted between thirty and seventy-five minutes. These can all be found on the *Fresh Out the Cocoon* website. The themes that resonated the most with my interviewees were found to be: (1) the journey to acceptance, (2) the "why" behind their service, and (3) the impact of doing their work while being fat and Black. Though they were interviewed about different topics, there is a common familial thread that I found to be both informative and inspiring. The following excerpts from interviews capture these moments when they were most salient. By the end of each of these interviews, there was no doubt in my mind that a fat Black collective has *always* been present. However, it is the lack of resources that has limited the magnetic force that pulls us all together. Good news! Our resources are multiplying.

HOW DID THE FAMILY ARRIVE AT FAT ACCEPTANCE?

In the preceding chapters, I laid out the journey that carried me to fat acceptance. Much of my arrival at this destination had to do with treatment I had received from others as well as internalized weight stigma. There were also moments of meeting special people who changed how I would forever see myself. My podcast changed me too! Here are a few of the lessons I learned from my sisters through speaking with them in interviews.

Chè Monique, founder of the Society of Fat Mermaids, highlighted tension in her relationship with her mother as it related to her weight. While she had a great childhood, she distinctly remembers being teased by young boys at school in relation to the fat she had on her arms. After spending some time in working to cover this up, she says she had an epiphany: "There was a day, and it hit me. You really cannot hide fat. . . . There's nothing I can do, put on, cover up that's going to make me look not fat."

Tiana Dodson, an international activist who is stationed in Germany, spoke about her project, The One Beautiful YES!, and remembered when she was constantly shut out of fitness spaces because of her size. After she found acceptance by playing into the "good fatty" archetype, fielding her involvement in physical fitness as the good and right thing fat folks should do, she realized she wanted something more. She also was still being bombarded by doctors and health care professionals to lose weight. She spoke about her journey to fat acceptance through this frustration: "So when I started practicing [as a fitness coach], and everybody who came to me was coming to me because they wanted to lose weight, it just always felt so hollow, because I, by that time, I had given up on the whole weight loss thing. . . . I was really just more interested and really just felt better about just working on my health. Who cared what the scales said."

Adrienne Ray, the owner of Curve Conscious in Philadelphia, also spoke about her experience and finding liberation while at college. She talked about her relationship with a fat friend who already had found acceptance. By conversing with her, the pieces to her own liberation started to fall in place: "I remember looking at her in awe. Like, this girl . . . and she was dark-skinned. And I was just like, she is stepping out in the world, fierce! Like, this is who I am. I'm cute. I don't care what you think. And I remember asking her about that, because I had such insecurity around certain parts of my body. . . . And when sis came out with the camisole on and some shorts, I was like, whoa! You doing this?!? And she was like, 'Girl, it's hot! . . . Yeah, I'm going out in a camisole. I don't care.' And that really like, opened my eyes."

Taken together, these excerpts from the podcast show that in many cases the treatment and struggles fat Black women face are somewhat universal. Whether it be the jokes made about us, the constant pushback from health care professionals, along with the rejection from particular spaces unless we conform, we are united through our lived experiences of piss-poor treatment. What also is evident is that there is always a forerunner somewhere present, helping to point us in the right direction. Some find that inspiration in childhood, while others may not know it exists until late in adulthood. In some cases, we are the forerunner (unbeknownst to us). Nevertheless, community serves as a vital component in the heartbeat of the fat Black experience.

THE "WHY" BEHIND WHAT THE SISTERS DO

Oftentimes on the podcast, discussion arose in relation to interviewees' motivation for their service or contribution back to the community. For many, even if they were involved in business, the motive for creating such was twofold: economic success and "paying it forward" to the fat Black community at large. Interviewees always expressed a need or desire to pass something to the next generation. They expressed a need to impact society for the good of fat acceptance.

For Jai Mobley of Fat Mermaids, the popularity of her "IDGAF About Your Diet Susan" design brought her to an "aha" moment in realizing that activism was at play. During our interview, she talked about the influence of that moment and her ultimate goal in launching the Fat Mermaids brand: ". . . That it just wasn't about the mermaids. That people really wanted to wear things that expressed how they feel. But it's all about making more and doing more for fat women and non-men people who don't see enough for themselves in the fashion industry."

Lastly, Aja B. Stubbs, founder of *Belle-Noir,* the first plus-size magazine for fat Black women, stopped by to talk about her dedication to the community: "I wanted to get more exposure. And so, that's part of what the heart of plus-size, what *Belle-Noir* was about when I first started it . . . just to give women of color a place to say, 'This is where we can come to see ourselves represented.'"

The theme of positively impacting communities and passing something on to those that follow in your footsteps is one that has been both lived and talked about through the podcast. Utilizing the concept of community and family, it's easy to see the work that fat Black women do as an inheritance they hope to give away some day. Through their service, we also see that they are creating legacies and passing them to other women in the community, removing the cishetero norms of where legacy comes from, and producing "mothers" like Brandi Wharton of Magical Fat Black Femmes. The future of fat Black excellence is nonbinary in this context. It is inclusive. It is queer. It is effective.

WHAT'S THE POWER OF DOING THIS WORK WHILE BLACK AND FAT?

The propensity to "All Lives Matter" fat acceptance by fat White people in the fat community is far and wide. It is the reason many fat Black folks decided to start their own groups and organizations. The willful blindness to acknowledge that living in a fat Black body has difficulties and barriers all its own not only devalues the movement for fat acceptance, but also builds opposition to progress in minority communities. The guests on the podcast did not mince words when considering what it means to do what they do in the identities they possess. There is strength in building communities that look like you. Interviewees were clear on this topic.

Ivy Felicia, The Body Relationship Coach™, spoke about the uniqueness of her lived experience as a Black fat woman, and the need to bring that to an online platform so that other women might find healing: "In the end of 2016, I started getting a lot of revelation and understanding around being a fat Black woman, and how that whole trifecta is very complex and it's unlike any other. Because you are discriminated against for being a true minority. You're Black. You're a woman. And you're fat. So, we definitely experience discrimination and challenges in a different way. . . . I just wanted to create a space online where other women of color who are fat could heal."

Malaika Salaam of Purple Hair and Converse brought all her energy to discuss who she is and why it is important for our community and the work she does: "I bring all of myself. The simplest way that I have broken that down. I'm Black. I'm fat. I'm queer, and I'm femme. Those are the important things that people need to know about me. . . . Those identifiers are very political, and that's very important for me because I do live my politics, and so I do want to put that out front so people know what they're getting. . . . I believe that my existence is resistance. I am a disrupter."

Dr. Lenese Stephens of Hopeful Counseling also spoke to this by making a point to identify herself clearly to clients and to communicate her commitment toward the community via her website. She explains: "In creating my website . . . I made sure that I put in my bio that my research is geared toward the plus-size community, and in essence of highlighting the quality of life for African American plus-size women. So knowing that is within my bio, and knowing that people can read that, I will say, I do have a large population of clients I serve that are plus-size women, and they definitely are seeking therapy and services of how to become more empowered."

In these excerpts, it is clear that by the simple identification of identities used within the Black fat community, family is located, resources are rendered, and minds are healed. When we state who we are, we're not playing "identity politics." When we state who we are, we are not playing the "race card." No. Rather, we are calling each other by name. To announce that you are Black, fat, queer, femme, and the like is sometimes the only magnetic force to those also looking to connect. It speaks of a particular lived experience shared, without ever having to expound. Now, this is not to say that we are all alike simply by these labels, but it is to say that those names and labels we use have enough similarities that seeking out additional information in these areas is warranted. It says that we can have peace in walking away from platforms that do not center us the same way. It says that these prospective spaces are places where labor is shared, and we will not be required to do all the heavy lifting.

Uniting with my fat Black family for the first time in this context was like a reunion. Whether it was sharing stories about dating fails with author and comedian Cecily Alexandria in episode 10 of season 2, or talking comics and the Usher scandal with Nichelle Gunby, founder of the website *Some Like It Nerdy!*, in episode 7, the connection we shared through our experiences of being fat and Black was real. The realization of our own community was just as present. I was struck by fascination, joy, and disbelief. It was kinda like the moment in *The Wiz*

(Internet Movie Database, n.d.) when Dorothy was about to go home, and Glinda the good witch was like:

Glinda: *Hello, Dorothy.*

Dorothy: *Please, is there a way for me to get back home?*

Glinda: *Well, Dorothy, you were wise and good enough to help your friends to come here and find what was inside them all the time. That's true for you, also.*

Dorothy: *Home? Inside of me? I don't understand.*

Glinda: *Home is a place we all must find, child. It's not just a place where you eat or sleep. Home is knowing. Knowing your mind, knowing your heart, knowing your courage. If we know ourselves, we're always home, anywhere.*

Allow me to translate . . .

So much seeking and questioning had brought me to a place of knowing. I had found my family. We had all been searching to find that place of comfort, by possibly never realizing that by searching and doing the work, we had also been creating these safe spaces within ourselves all along. We had been building homes for ourselves and for others to find refuge in. This was the knowing. I realized that in locating my family, I actually located myself. In bringing life to others, I was actually saving my own.

7

TOGETHER WE CAN CHANGE THE WORLD

AN ODE TO FAT. BLACK. GIRL. MAGIC.

The year was 1964. The Mississippi Freedom Democratic Party had attended the Democratic National Convention held in Atlantic City, New Jersey. It was Fannie Lou Hamer's turn to speak. Hamer, a full-figured, dark-skinned Black woman deeply involved in liberation efforts, took her seat and opened her mouth. The stories she told would speak of the horrors of the segregated South (NBC 1964). She would speak of the beatings of those who were arrested with her. She would talk about the sacrifices she made simply to claim her right to vote.

Born to parents Ella and James Townsend, Hamer was the baby girl of twenty children (Mills 2007). Intelligent, literate, and partially disabled, she attended school for most of her childhood, leaving to work on a plantation through sharecropping at the age of twelve (Mills 2007). She would continue learning through reading the Bible, and later using these concepts to connect to the struggle for the liberation of Black people. Fannie Lou Hamer, a fierce activist, is most known for her speech at the Democratic National Convention, but if you were to stop there, you'd miss the pain and triumph in her story. You'd miss the magic that makes us shine when the world turns its back to our struggle.

Mama Hamer learned to be, among many things, a supplier of goods and resources. She was a leader and manager, creating the Freedom Farm Cooperative and the Pig Project to ensure we'd all eat (Asch 2008). She was a devoted mother and shelter for others, adopting two girls with her husband, and purchased land for housing stability. She was an author who wrote her autobiography. She was a grassroots politician (Mills 2007). All of these things were achieved WHILE Hamer lived in a fat, disabled body. Her focus was on what many fat activists and supporters of fat acceptance speak on today. Equal rights, equitable partnerships, and food that fed the body and soul without the weight loss BS.

She is who we see when we hear the names of Makia Green with Black Lives Matter DC, the "Dreams and Schemes" fund, Working Families Party, and BWF (Black Womxn For Team). International activists like Jill Andrew stand on her shoulders, advocating for fat bodies through the lens of human rights and implementing initiatives like Body Confidence Awareness Week in Canada, the Bite Me! film festival for young girls, and countless other initiatives that have rendered her special recognition for gender equality, LGBTQ+ rights, and body acceptance. Hamer was the forerunner for those involved in organizations like Acta Non Verba: Youth Urban Farm Project with Kelly Carlisle, the Young Women's Freedom Center with Ifasina TaMeicka L. Clear, the Positive Results Corporation with Kandee Lewis, and the California National Organization for Women with Kolieka Seigle as president.

Hamer was the embodiment of Fat Black Girl Magic before the term existed. Her legacy, alive and well, now translated through the lives of other fat Black women, is making a difference today.

For those invested in the power of stories, the inspiration drawn from our very own, Toni Morrison, leaves us breathless. There has been no doubt that Morrison wrote for a Black audience. She said so herself. Beginning as an editor in 1965 at Random House, Morrison would later go on to publish her first novel, *The Bluest Eye,* in 1970, at the age of thirty-nine (Als 2003). Over the span of her career, she received numerous awards, including the Nobel Prize and Pulitzer Prize. She served as the Robert F. Goheen Chair in the Humanities at Princeton University (Als 2003). She was an academic and a scholar, fiercely dedicated to the enrichment of Black lives through her work. Mama Morrison wanted us to imagine our realities without White influence. She wanted us to see ourselves through decolonized eyes.

We hear her influence today in books like *Blue Talk and Love* by Mecca Jamilah Sullivan. Her no-nonsense discussion on the politics of race, the Black body, and its implications can also be found all over writings like *So You Want to Talk about Race* by Ijeoma Oluo, Roxane Gay's *Hunger,* Tressie McMillan Cottom's *THICK,* Brittney C. Cooper's *Eloquent Rage: A Black Feminist Discovers Her Superpower,* and Tamara Winfrey Harris's *The Sisters Are Alright: Changing the Broken Narrative of Black Women in America.*

Toni Morrison showed us that we did have to appeal to the majority to validate our beauty. In all of her fat Black glory, she taught us not to forget about our own. She is the essence of affirmations written by confidence coach Erica Ware, the self-love letters composed by Stacie Evans, and the comprehensive, unapologetic essays of Sonya Renee Taylor and Ashleigh Shackelford. In Toni Morrison, we see ourselves.

If you love Lizzo, you ought to love Willie Mae "Big Mama" Thornton. Born in 1926 and brought up in the Black church, Big Mama took her talents on the road with the Hot Harlem Revue, singing and playing the drums and harmonica. She is most famously known for HER hit, "Hound Dog," later repurposed by Elvis. Mama Thornton was not ashamed of her frame as she proudly proclaimed to be 300 pounds. She reminds us that we can be multitalented without having to shrink ourselves. She was a queen and pioneer of R&B music, topping the charts and touring all over the country. We hear her influence today in the soulful sounds of Cocoa Venus.

Performers have a way of digging deep in their souls to pull out something beautiful. The dark, inappropriate, and forbidden can be used as a position of empowerment to explain and educate. I'm grateful for those like Irene McCalphin, Miasia Raqasat, Juicy D. Light, Arika Armstrong, Naima Niambi, and Mollena Lee Williams-Haas who harness this power and give magic in a way that reaches those on the margins. They remind us we're not forgotten. They remind us that we're full of value.

Y'all remember Shirley and "Mama" from *What's Happening!!* Shirley Ann Hemphill was an aspiring comedian when she landed the role of Shirley for the show (Denise 1999), and Mabel King had just finished taping *The Wiz* (I Love Old School Music 2018). Both would illustrate strength on and off the set. Shirley's character was funny, a business owner, and a good friend. I looked up to her when I was younger. My six-year-old self did not see the puns in her appearance. I did not pay attention to the difference between her physique and that of Nadine on *What's Happening Now!!* I'm grateful that writers in her case got it right! She was a fat Black woman who unapologetically wore her natural hair and was thriving economically while still having empathy. Today, comedians like Cecily Alexandria, Erica Watson, and Nikki Bailey help to carry the torch.

Mabel King, on the other hand, was already well known and was looking to push the boundaries of what successful Black TV shows looked like during the '70s. Mabel reportedly walked off the set of *What's Happening!!*, ending her tenure due to the lack of progression from the show producers (I Love Old School Music 2018). She also would change scripts during recording to ensure positive depictions of the Black family. Mabel also wanted to remain plus-size as a performer and actress. We see today a melding of Mabel's aspirations and Shirley's character traits in the productions of greats like Samantha Irby and Erin Sharkey.

There is no end to the Black fat model magic that is happening on platforms like Instagram, BUT if you are not following OGs like Saucyé West, can you even say that you are living?!? Born Antoinette Tameka Cloird, Saucyé has been in the fashion industry for roughly nine years. Drawing inspiration from her mother, Brenda, Saucyé was raised to wear what she felt good in, irrespective of the size of her body. This has led to her shutting runways down with style and grace! An advocate of fat acceptance, Saucyé started the hashtag #fatandfree and refuses to partner with any company who does not offer sizes above a 4X. Like her, models Simone Mariposa, La'Shaunae Steward, Mojo Disco, and Geneieve Gilmore serve looks for days! And how can we forget those that keep product so we can stay fly and rep our beliefs without shame. Thanks and gratitude to Neish Cromwell of Carefree Fat Girl, Alex Bee of PlushWishes, Shawnda Harper of the Nappy Nerd, Letitia Young of Honey's Child Boutique, and Adrienne Ray, holding down the ONLY plus-size consignment shop in Philly, Curve Conscious.

And where would we be without our healers? Those that sit with us, cry with us, and remind us to breathe. Those that know what to say and how to say it to get us moving again in the right direction. I show gratitude to mothers like Brandi Wharton,

Ta'lor L. Pinkston, and Celeste Smith, who house whole communities of Black fat femmes and womxn under their wings. They remind us that mothers are not kin to just those who come from their wombs. We also have the aunties, sisters, and cousins who love us to life through their practice like Ivy Felicia, Y Falami Devoe, and Alysha Navarro-Henry. Chefs Oya Woodruff and Fresh Sharonmelissa Roberson heal us through food, while others heal through movement.

Gracious, hard, and gritty movement all rest here in our community. Big Girl Barbell led by Olympic powerlifter Amanda Gilliam is a good example of inner strength manifesting itself in our bodies. Accessibility advocate Courtney Marshall uses her commitment to accessible fitness to reach many through classes in water aerobics and Zumba. Dianne Bondy, Jessica Jade, Andréa Ranae Johnson, Latoya Shauntay Snell, and Mirna Valerio all dispel the myths of what fat bodies cannot do. Ebony Smith, Etang Inyang, and Tammy Johnson do the same in their own way. You can catch them running marathons, doing headstands while practicing yoga, or using art forms like bellydancing to connect their bodies back to movement.

Last but not least, this ode would be incomplete without our educators. Those who have taken the time to synthesize information and make it palatable are invaluable. I stand on the shoulders of individuals like Leslie Graham-Wilson, a longtime supporter of fat acceptance, teaching in Jersey City, New Jersey, and Tigress Osborn, a staple in fat acceptance across the San Francisco Bay Area in California, both being educators whose commitment to fat liberation has lasted over twenty years. Awesome writers like Hess Love also come to mind, as they create and frame arguments in a way that makes us see the world anew. Jamie Patterson and Ellise Smith educate through photography, capturing the beauty and essence of the fat Black experience. Bernadette Gailliard-Mayabi, Desiree Lynn Adaway, Stephanie

Chrismon, and E-K Daufin & Associates all offer consultation services to educate and inspire.

As I look around, I'd argue there isn't one thing in this world that Black fat women have not done. Not one. We are a force of nature that has been moving and keeping things afloat throughout time. Anyone arguing that fat girls can't, won't, or don't do great things is lying. We move. We sing. We draw. We inspire and change lives. Together we can change the world! Together the world . . . OUR world . . . is already changing!

8

NOW THAT WE'RE HERE, WHAT'S NEXT?

TWELVE DAYS ABROAD
WITH HUMAN MIRRORS

In July of 2019, I took a deep breath as I stared at the screen. Several times before this, I had mulled over in my mind the idea of taking a solo trip, but on this particular day, I was ready to commit. I decided to make a phone call to ASAP Tickets and have someone else find me the best tickets for my trip. When I finally reached a representative, I gave her the details of my travel. I planned to take a trip over the Christmas holiday into the new year. She found me nonstop flights round-trip out of JFK. We went over the details of my passport several times before the booking was official. Then my itinerary was set. I'd be traveling for the first time to West Africa. Dakar, Senegal, to be exact. ALONE. I was nervous but also excited. I was ready for a new adventure and was tired of waiting for the "right" time to take the leap.

2019 was a year of significance for Black Americans who wanted to visit the western part of the continent. It was slated as the Year of Return by Ghanaian president Nana Akufo-Addo to mark the 400th anniversary of the first slave ship leaving from Africa. As a result, West Africa saw one of the biggest influxes of Black American tourism to places like Ghana and Nigeria. I, however, sought to be different. I wanted this trip to be something meaningful that included the activities I wanted to participate in. I was hoping to not go full tourist during my trip, but to really experience the culture of Dakar. To be frank, I wanted the non-Westernized version of West Africa, not the version often presented to Americans to help offset the stereotypes we hear about the region. I decided that if I was going to travel, I'd go to Ghana or Nigeria at a later date due to these reasons. I wanted to be immersed with the people in the city. I set out to practice French (the official language of Dakar) and dabbled a little in Wolof (the official indigenous language of Dakar) in preparation for my trip.

A few weeks before I was set to travel, I spoke with my tour guide, who reassured me that I would have a great time in the city. He also kept mentioning to me that making the decision to travel to Dakar was significant, because it was me "coming home." He spoke about the accommodations that would be made for me in areas I visited. He talked about how he was happy to take me around the city, at no additional cost, to "meet the family." Hearing him say these things gave me all the feels. Here I was, a Black American woman who had never spent more than six hours on a flight, preparing to travel across the Atlantic Ocean to be around people who *already* considered me to be "family." They did not know who I was. They were not aware of my work in fat activism. They knew nothing of my accolades. Just by virtue of our skin color being the same, with a shared history of the slave trade, I was being welcomed back to a place

where my ancestors may have never been. To say I was smitten
is an understatement. I believed his words and hung onto them
as I washed clothes and stuffed my luggage. I looked forward to
being reunited with "family" I had never met.

All of the excitement about Dakar almost had me forgetting
the extra labor of what it took to prepare a fat body like mine
for flights. One of the downsides of booking a flight with a representative on the phone was that I was not able to research the
airline or look at the pictures of the plane. Currently, Southwest
is the only airline that has a customer of size (COS) policy that
accommodates larger bodies by providing additional seating at
no additional cost with a preboarding option. If I were flying
with Southwest, my anxiety would have been reduced to null. I
would have rested in the fact that I would be flying to Dakar in
the most comfortable setup available. I would not have worried
about being able to stretch my legs or allowing my hips to spread.
I would not have remembered all the times before when I ran the
risk of bruising due to my body being smushed against armrests
that didn't give. And then there were the people. The people who
sigh when they walk up to their seat and see that you are sitting
beside them. The people who insist that the armrests stay down.
Also, the people who do their best to create dividers between
your body and theirs, yet find a way to make your body an extra
cushion when they sleep. I so hated this process! It wasn't until
after I booked did I receive an email from Delta to complete the
details of my flight. Thankfully, there was at least an aisle seat
available. After having suffered a pulmonary embolism in 2015,
I knew I needed this to make getting up and moving my legs
easier. I booked this quickly and hoped that I would not be on a
full flight going and returning. After all, who flies on Christmas
Eve?! With my fingers crossed, I started to imagine that perhaps
my experience of meeting "family" would start before I ever left
this country. I imagined that the same folks going to Dakar when

I was would be happy to share a row of seats with a new family member. The reality of what I encountered was not as fluffy, but it wasn't hostile. The person I shared the row with was pleasant, although they did not lift the armrest between us. My armrest, however, did go up, which prevented my hips from bruising on the 7½-hour-long flight. I ate the provided snacks in my lap, because I've never been able to have the serving tray down while I'm sitting. The flight attendants were kind. I was handed my requested seat belt extender discreetly with a smile at the beginning of the flight.

Arriving in Dakar, I started to see what so many Black Americans envision as "paradise." Spaces without White people! I think the last White person I saw for the first forty-eight hours of my trip was the pilot as I was leaving the plane. My co-travelers were Black. Security? Black. Taxi drivers? BLACK. I even saw a few dogs as we drove away from the airport, and I'm almost certain, although their fur was speckled with tans and creams, they too were Black on the inside. So many hues of chocolate! So much unfeigned beauty! I was in awe of the people. I was in awe of the development of the city. Dakar's highways were better than some in the States. The city is lined with beaches and palm trees. The architecture of buildings was breathtaking. I quickly started to see the differences in advertising as we drove past billboards. The people represented on them were Black. Black and happy. Black and fashionable. Black and universal. There was no niche market. Those Black billboards were for everyone, and everyone in Dakar was Black! As I pondered the impacts of this, I was enveloped in the hospitality of the city. My hosts were all welcoming. The people I encountered on the streets called me "sister." I knew by now that most of what we'd heard about Africa and its people had been a lie, but to experience it for myself was life changing. Stories filled with exaggerations of loss, ignorance, and savagery had long been shared by the United States, but also had grown old for anyone who had the slightest interest to learn more about the continent. I wondered if this was the reason the United States spread the lies about the continent? The idea that one day, one day Black Americans would muster up enough courage to visit the land we were stolen from probably petrified the majority, knowing that with the proper resources, it wouldn't take much for us to build our own empires abroad and stop putting up with the bullshit that is White supremacy. I pondered. By day two, I had an awareness about myself and the place (at least the one I was generalizing to every other place in Africa I had not been) that had been white-washed in lack and slander. I was ready to meet the fam! I was ready to accept being accepted.

Heading out into the streets of the city was quite an ordeal. Taxis filled the road alongside motorbikes, buses, pedestrians, and sometimes animals. Traditional clothing made for a colorful scenery. Yellows, pinks, blues, and greens set against the dark skin of Dakar natives were picture perfect. No filter needed. And these colors were not just reserved for those in smaller bodies. Fat women draped these colors against their skin as well. In Dakar, fashion was not just reserved for folks with smaller frames. In fact, I learned that larger bodies were preferable in many cases for men, by the honks of horns from passing taxis as I walked down the street, the efforts made by them to offer their contact info despite me speaking no French, and the downright forwardness of others to introduce themselves at whim, shooting their shot with no regard for the company I was in. As a fat Black woman, it would have been easy to get lost in the gaze of men who found me desirable simply for the shape of my body. I was finding acceptance arguably quicker than I did in the States. In a matter of hours, I knew I could get clothes that would fit me the way I wanted without having to compromise on styles. I also knew if I wanted a "boo," that could be arranged as well!

Up until this point, I had experienced no difference in treatment in service due to my size. So, what was the catch?

I'd quickly start to learn on the third day of my trip. While traveling to Gorée, an island off the coast of Dakar where slaves were once sold, my tour guide began to speak a bit more frankly about relations in Dakar. During my first day, he had given me a brief history of the government and how leadership under the current president was causing Dakar to suffer. He spoke about corruption and mistreatment, but I'm sure I couldn't hear him fully over all the representation I was taking in. On our way to the island, he had to haggle our way to the port with a taxi driver who was not flexible in the price to take us. For reference, *everything* in Dakar can be negotiated. When we finally scored a ride, my tour guide expressed that one of the drawbacks of Dakar was that "even your own people try to take advantage of you." This was a sobering moment for me, because if you'd let me tell it, according to the "pro-Black" delegation of the United States, representation and financial mobility are all that we need to excel as a people. I started to think to myself, what is there to be said of a people who look like you, have the ability to rule, and still find ways to disenfranchise their members? It was almost ironic that this was taking place as we were headed to the House of Slaves museum to learn about the history of the slave trade in Senegal, the roles of Senegal's inhabitants in its perpetuation, and the events that brought us to where we are in the present day. Despite the history published around the museum and the stories about slavery that may have been exaggerated as they relate to the island in hopes to boost tourism in the area, one thing Dakar residents do not shy away from is the role Senegalese people played in the slave trade.

While in Dakar, there seemed to be a keen awareness of and accountability for the slave trade that happened on the people's watch. While this didn't change the fact that I was standing as a representation of the descendant of slaves who made it back to the continent to pay homage in a way to those who did not, it did help to possibly explain the type of hospitality I had been experiencing. Perhaps this was a way that residents compensated for the treatment that was doled out in the past? Could it be that the rejection of old was being replaced by acceptance in the now to make amends? At times, it definitely seemed that way. What also seemed clear was the fact that White folk who were sparingly present throughout my trip had not received the memo. I'm not sure why this surprised me, but the disdain for their presence overrode the hurt I acknowledged from learning the role of the Senegalese in the slave trade. Wherever they were, they were there "White peopling." I watched as they stood to smile for pictures on the steps of the very place slaves were sold. I experienced their entitlement to stand in the way of the Door of No Return (known as the last place in the port where slaves would pass before being loaded onto ships to be transported in slavery). They shushed people at exhibits when they couldn't hear, despite those people being Black, who, at least in my opinion, had a greater right to be present than they did. Looking back, White people became the glaring villain in the story of my travels, albeit their presence was few and far between.

Circling back to the issues of inequality and corruption, I find that Dakar is a great site for analysis relating to the Black American experience in all of its forms. As a fat Black woman, I experienced a welcoming in the city that I do not get in the States even among my own community members. I was not treated differently due to my skin color or size, BUT that does not mean that difference in treatment does not happen. While we here in the United States love to speak much about income inequality and representation, I found it mind-boggling that I was in the presence of people who had both income and representation, and yet many residents still suffer due to poverty and crime.

And I don't point this out as a discovery that most of us do not know. "All skinfolk ain't kinfolk" is a long-standing proverb in the Black community that has alerted us for generations about those who look like us but are not loyal to what it really means to be a positive influence to the community. However, in this instance, the analysis is slightly different, because at least in the United States most of the inequality we deal with can be seen rather openly through the funnel of White supremacy. In the case of what may be happening in places like Dakar, this too could be the case, but you only see it through a peripheral lens. For example, when traveling in and out of the city center, drivers are bombarded by vendors in the road selling everything from peanuts to coat hangers. I learned from my host that this is actually illegal in the city, but due to the lack of employment, people use this avenue to earn money for their families. There are so many vendors participating in this act that the crime becomes normalized. As a result, no one is arrested or accosted due to selling goods illegally. Looking at this issue through a micro lens, it would be hard to see the role that the government may play in economics. It would be even harder to see the influence of White supremacy on the employment and economics of Dakar; but I can assure you the influence of the West is present, and where there is influence, White supremacy is never far behind.

My experience in Dakar was also highlighted by the treatment I received due to other reasons. As my vacation continued, I started to be able to tell the difference in the treatment I received due to the fact that I was American. I chuckled with residents as they volunteered to be taken back to the States. I watched others raise prices for items and ask for money in US dollars. On one occasion, I visited a local nail shop to have a manicure and pedicure done. When a song by Beyoncé came on the radio and I began to sing along, an employee from the salon walked over to the system and turned the song off. The look on the receptionist's face said it all. Yes, I looked like them, but I was in Senegal, not America! I should stay in my place and run my riffs at home.

REPRESENTATION IS GREAT, BUT STRUCTURAL CHANGE IS BETTER

Taking my experience in from being in Dakar challenged a lot of what is often debated in the United States about what Black folk need and what will move the needle forward toward our liberation. So much of what I see today focuses on representation, and rightly so. I believe that we need to see marginalized groups represented everywhere, because they are an active part of our society. We need to see more fat Black performers, artists, organizers, moms, and friends. We need to break stereotypes around the idea that fat Black womxn make less desirable mates. We need to be willing to confront our own biases and let people live out loud in their own truths. Representation is great. But just as I saw in Dakar, it doesn't equate to structural change. Seeing someone on a billboard has a whole lot less impact if that person is underpaid and unable to afford basic needs. And I'm not saying that we have to choose one over the other. We need BOTH to fully thrive.

So, where does this leave us fat Black girls? Where does it leave our "allies"? What can we do today to help us in the fight against fatphobia and all of the "isms" that accompany it? We keep fighting. We keep shining a light for those coming up behind us. We keep making stands at the family gatherings. We keep representing. Representation opens the door for change. It starts conversations about who is missing from the table and who needs to be included. We ALL need to be included. It also opens up the possibility of new ideas and innovation. The Black community does not have to follow in the footsteps of White folks' leadership. Especially when we are dealing interpersonally with one another. What need do we have for White-supremacist ideas in our intimate gatherings? Can we not carve out a sacred place for us to dwell away from the bullshit so we can run a new community in spite of the oppression happening around us?

We do not have to peddle the same religious beliefs. We do not have to hold one another to the same rigid standards. We should drop the idea that working twice as hard to be considered good enough applies to us when we are in the company of one another. What place do these standards have here? We should love our people whose skin has been enriched with twice as much melanin the same as those who have been favored by the masses because of their lighter shade. Big bodies should thrive in our neighborhoods the way that smaller ones do. What is stopping us from creating this paradise within our own living quarters?

By confronting our own shit, we can get free. Make no mistake, we ALL have shit to confront. I'm still confronting my shit daily. No one should skip this step. And this is not the "healthy" type of shit that comes out in one push. You know, the type of shit that you can easily clean up with a napkin or wipe. No, this type of shit I'm talking about is that messy, yellow to orange to greenish type shit that runs up and down babies' backs. This is the shit that makes you question whether or not you have a virus or are coming down with the flu. It's the type of shit no one wants to touch if they had the choice. It's the kind you dread if you have to deal with it because there's no escaping the impending doom of cleanup.

Within the piles of that messy shit lies our freedom. It forces us to look at it, smell it, and clean it up. We will not like what we'll see. We will not want to sit and deal with the smell. But I promise it will make us better. It will help us to identify our missteps. It will help us be kinder and gentler with one another as we are trying to get a grasp on this thing called life. Dealing with our shit will help us to cast off the indoctrination we simply do not need. To free ourselves from White-supremacist ideas, getting new knowledge is key; but we cannot decide what knowledge is worth casting off *until* we confront our shit.

To be clear, this is not a swooping blanket statement to be used in all conversations. I'm not suggesting that we pull ourselves up by our own bootstraps to create social change. I'm also not talking about governmental change here. I'm talking about governing how we treat one another on an interpersonal level. By facing our own "demons" of ableist, fatphobic, homophobic, and transphobic ideologies, we can deal with ourselves in hopes of making our neighbors' lives easier. There is a magic in being able to respond to one another in love. One right response can heal decades of wrong ones. Liberation flourishes where safety and trust reside. We do not need government for this. We need knowledge, understanding, and a willingness to see one another free.

And no one should think that there is no capacity in which they can serve as an ally (or whatever term one feels comfortable using). We all can. We all have something that can be leveraged on behalf of another. Whether it is power, an encouraging word, speaking up for those being mistreated, or good ol' fashioned money, we can make something happen for others. Learning to be more flexible, to change our focus from what is being given to what we can give, will allow us to continue in the traditions of those who have come before us, fostering hope and connection with our sisters who stand beside us on this battlefield of non-ending bullshit.

Acknowledging that the bullshit is non-ending, I'd also like to take this time to encourage us to take care of ourselves. Get rest. Laugh hard. Cry. Find spaces that allow you to be unapologetically yourself *even* if it's only for a few hours. Take breaks.

Martyrdom is a tired trope when it comes to fat Black women. We do not have to kill ourselves for the collective. If anything, the collective needs to see us living more than anything else. They need to pull from the wisdom of our lived experiences. They need to be able to see that things change and get better. And we need to believe that we were not born only to serve others. We serve in love, but there will always be more to us than that.

Change within these microstructures would do wonders for us fat Black girls! We could breathe better, sleep better, and be fat in peace. Research studies detail that weight stigma is more harmful than weight itself. Give us the chance to thrive. Give us the chance to create. Give us the chance to live in a community that doesn't think less of us because centuries-long rumors have been spread insisting that looking like us means we're less than. Believe that the love that flows from our hearts to our work and to our family is steeped in the same blood of ancestors often talked about in triumphant and spectacular ways. In us lies the same magic of dynasties that have come before us. We are necessary parts of the puzzle. Not mirages. Parts.

CONCLUSION

A LOVE LETTER
TO FAT GIRLS IN
BLACK BODIES

Dear Sisters,

My beautiful and wonderfully made sisters. I do hope that this book has spoken to some part of you. I hope that you see yourself in the pages of labored love. To know you is to love you. You weather storms that make others wonder how you made it out alive. The rhythm of your walk is infused with magic even when you're standing or sitting still. I want you to know that things get better. I want you to know that if you're reading this book, you have survived 100 percent of your worst days. Healing happens, but it doesn't happen overnight. Give it time, sis. Watch the sun come out again for you. Watch love show up unexpectedly and sweep you off your feet.

Pay attention to community. We love us. Pay attention to those who shout out the most marginalized among us. We love us. Never conform for a minute of acceptance. That shit is fleeting and will leave you empty. Never dim your life in expectation of inclusion so someone else can shine. That shit is fleeting and will leave you empty.

Laugh loud. Take up space. Wear that bodycon and crop top. At least when folks take pictures in hopes of shaming you, your smile will light up the room. Joy looks good on you. Always carry your own supply. Don't pass mirrors too quickly. Even you should know how beautiful you are.

Know that this world is socially constructed, made from the co-creating of communication. Use your language, your behaviors, your words to create something for yourself. Know that you're never alone. Even if you never see us, we out here. Even if you never feel us, we out here.

Walk with confidence of the work that you've inwardly done. Unpacking is necessary if thriving is your goal. Unpacking will help you walk away from things that no longer serve you without feeling bad. Unpacking will help you differentiate what is you and what is being projected by others. Unpacking will have you knowing yourself and being okay with whatever those results show. Don't be afraid of the outcome. You still breathing, right? Then there's still time for change.

Take ALL the compliments. Don't sell yourself short. It's okay to be a big damn deal. It's okay to be sexy, fine, chill, and fascinating. Sometimes you will be the magic that others cannot explain. Don't try to put it in words. Leave them folks in awe.

Never forget to move in empathy. You will meet people who know less. You will meet people who know more. Be gentle with both. Empathy is not a justification for abuse. Get up from the table when love is no longer being served.

I promise you things get better. Just like your glow up after high school.

I hope this book has spoken to you. I hope it has resonated and put some of your fears to rest. The world is cold, but our community is warm. Don't shy away from the fire. Embrace it.

Love,
Joy

AFTERWORD

By Dr. Jill Andrew, PhD

*D*r. Joy Arlene Renee Cox, THANK YOU! *Fat Girls in Black Bodies: Creating Communities of Our Own* is the "Ode to Fat. Black. Girl. Magic." we need to not only survive the onslaught of thin-centric, fatphobic misogynoir aimed squarely at our minds, bodies, and souls, but to help us both navigate and thrive through the stubbornness of belonging. Our fatness, our Blackness, and our *womxness* is the physical embodiment of socially constructed otherness courtesy of Eurocentric beauty ideals emboldened by the blueprint of white supremacy. Too many of us have had to engage on one hand in a heightened awareness—a "triple consciousness"—of our size, gender, and race corporeality while on the other hand our unruly bodies talk back, disrupt, and take up space unapologetically.

Audre Lorde was right—we are powerful and dangerous. We expose the fragility of the so-called mainstream. Dr. Cox's *Fat Girls in Black Bodies* gives us permission to not seek validation, to not belong, to fit out of constraining spaces and to reimagine fat Black time and space. The messiness of respectability politics coupled with the everyday and systemic weight of oppression threatens to control our rolls and plays out in the structural rules that too many of us have been beaten down by—the girdle, the corset, the "good" and the "bad" body archetype—manifestations of perceived responsible and irresponsible, moral and immoral, productive and unproductive citizenship judged by a waist size. *Fat Girls in Black Bodies* provides the framework for re-mirroring and re-remembering our own communities in our own image(s) so we may see ourselves through unfiltered, decolonized eyes and hopefully begin to see each other across borders.

Dr. Cox's publication has come to fruition during the United Nations' International Decade for People of African Descent (2015–2024). The major themes of the decade are recognition, justice, and development. We still continue to advocate for our due recognition as a unique people in all aspects of public life. "Justice" remains rather elusive for far too many of us, whether in the workplace, the classroom, the courtroom, or on the sidewalk jogging while Black, eating candy while Black, shopping while Black, regardless of the size of your bank account (Oprah can attest to that). Development, we've made our strides. We have begun to take stock of our Black dollars, our economic efficacy, though it still leaves our community faster than most. So where does fatness fit into all of this?

Our fat bodies are often read as unrecognizable, unjust, and overdeveloped so much so that many Black fat (or "phat") girls experience the toll of adultification in schools, where they are punished more severely than their white counterparts for the same behavior and assumed to be bigger and therefore wiser, more culpable, and are un-afforded the right to be a child. Fat bodies are still being price gouged in the plus-size fashion industry where sartorial choices remain predominantly feminized and priced well beyond straight sizes. And never underestimate the power of clothing. Our dressed bodies "present" us, but also make us present. Attire is a second skin and it's a key stakeholder in how we carry ourselves through this world. Our skin inevitably thickens for those of us who trouble and queer fashion's size, gender identity, and gender expression norms, who would much rather wear a tailored suit, blazer, or wingtip shoes. Fashion makes our performance real, at least temporarily.

As we emerge into our Black fat womxness, our assertiveness is mistaken for aggression, our passion for savagery—uncontrollable—and before you know it your colleague is intimidated or tone-policing you and the person you've trained is now your boss, and should you be anything but jovial and grateful, all hell might break loose. Black fatness is quickly labelled as unjust and unwarranted—unnecessary. *Fat Girls in Black Bodies* takes us through a journey of what it's like to travel through worlds, through relationships—familial and otherwise—in an invisible yet still hypervisible body where pain and joy are too often pitted against each other as dichotomous, when in fact their tensions often sit together. Our "overdeveloped" bodies are often denied health care, denied food, denied love, affordable housing, and other social supports because of the assumption of fatness somehow being synonymous with abundance and with "having enough."

As Black peoples, as African peoples, we must continue to fight collectively for our access to autonomy, to body justice, and for our fatness—yes, I said it. Our fight against fat stigma, anti-Black racism, and gender inequity must be intersectional—it must intersect everything from "common-sense" media violence to state-sanctioned violence. We cannot disaggregate our bodies from the world. *Fat Girls in Black Bodies* is political and personal. It provides a "how-to" guide to help inform our protests for our social, cultural, and economic recognition; for justice; and for our development as fat, Black womxn, while also rolling out the red carpet for the party in the meantime because, after all, no protest can happen without the party. It will help you "level up" your body consciousness with yourself. That is praxis. That *is* self-care.

What you do with *Fat Girls in Black Bodies* after you've read it through is up to you, but the one thing you won't be able to do is leave it on your bookshelf. Allies, you don't need to fully understand it or even identify with it, and we're certainly not looking for your validation or justification. Just take it in, listen, reflect, add it to your syllabi if you're an educator, and based on what you've taken away from reading, be willing to fall back or step up—be willing to risk something. When the chance presents itself for you to truly demonstrate allyship, step into discomfort (just like those bloody airplane armrests!).

For those of us for whom *Fat Girls in Black Bodies* was written, it will travel with you. Its wit, its grit, its at times bellyful humor, its painful jabs, and its memories will reflect many of your own experiences as a "Fat Black Girl" navigating communities, moving in and out of spaces, and making places of your own. Its perfect imperfections and its conversational tone laced with cautionary tales will travel with you. It will travel with you as much as the words and narratives of a parent, caring adult, teacher, or lover that broke you down or lifted you up. It will take you through the curves, the folds, the untouchable and the lush parts of who you are. It will be visceral. Dr. Cox is right, "revisiting your survival also means revisiting your pain." Put your feet up and dig in.

AFTERWORD

By Dr. Bernadette M. Gailliard-Mayabi, PhD

I must begin with saying THANK YOU, JOY! I hope I can speak on behalf of many, if not all, fat Black womxn when I say thank you for sharing our stories with the world. We are beautifully complex womxn whose experiences deserve a voice and I appreciate how you affirm and support us while helping to lead the charge for liberation. As Iyanla Vanzant would say, thank you for "calling a thing a thing" and standing bravely in your conviction and commitment to walk in your truth. I felt seen throughout this book. You had me recalling the messages I heard in church, from my family, and at school . . . then fondly reflecting on the places and the people with whom I feel accepted as my full self. Thank you for the opportunity to explore and interrogate my experiences while engulfed in your story and for feeling supported by the community you have helped to create.

As I reflect on the stories shared and insights offered from both research and the *Fresh Out the Cocoon* podcast, I most resonate with a question posed in chapter 4: "What's so hard about learning, people?" This is a powerful question. As an educator and coach, I recognize that learning has levels to it and, with this book, Dr. Cox is calling for all of us to go to a higher (and deeper) level of learning.

Consider one of the most recognized learning models: Bloom's Taxonomy. This model has six levels: (1) remember, (2) understand, (3) apply, (4) analyze, (5) evaluate, and (6) create. At the foundational levels (1 and 2), the focus is on recalling facts, summarizing information, and explaining and interpreting meaning. These things are not hard. But, to answer the question, the hard part about learning is when you advance to the higher levels (3–6) and are asked to apply what you have learned to real-life situations that are messy and complex. In relation to this book, the hard part is for us to embody the knowledge we have acquired through both study and experience in ways that allow us to know ourselves better, generate new possibilities, critique the status quo, and forge new pathways for ourselves and others.

So, I want to take this opportunity to explore what it might look like if we heeded Dr. Cox's call—if fat Black womxn and those who truly love us chose to take our learning to the next level and embody what we have learned in this book and throughout our lives.

First, let me talk to my sisters. Dr. Cox has opened up the space for us to have important conversations with ourselves and others about identity and acceptance. In the identity literature, there is a distinction made between avowed and ascribed identities. Avowed identities are the identity groups to which you say you belong, whereas ascribed identities are the groups others put you in (mostly based on generalizations and stereotypes). It is important to recognize that there may be a difference in how others perceive you, but you have the power to proudly proclaim your identities—whatever they may be and however the intersections work for you. Others do not get to tell you who you are, and when they try to, you have permission to call them out and tell them that they are wrong.

In order to strengthen these understandings about yourself, I invite you to have the hard conversations. Ask yourself:

- Who am I?

- Which identities do I avow and claim as my own and which have been ascribed to me?

- How does making the choice to accept or reject certain identities change the way I see myself?

- How do the intersections of the identities I value allow me to be the amazing, beautiful person I am?

Likewise, think about the beliefs that you have about yourself and how you "should" be, what you "should" do, and what you "should" have as you move in the world. Ask yourself:

- Where do these beliefs come from?

- Why do I think it "should" be this way?

- Are these beliefs still serving me?

- What truths exist to affirm who I am and help me grow in confidence and self-love?

It may take work with a therapist or coach and you might also engage practices such as journaling or yoga to develop these mindset shifts, but I believe it is necessary on the path to acceptance and joy that Dr. Cox describes.

This path also includes practicing radical self care. Throughout the book, Dr. Cox juxtaposes the messages we receive from people like family, preachers, and the media with the messages we tell ourselves personally and within the community. Then, she explicitly tells us, "by confronting our own shit, we can get free." This is calling on us to go deeper by not only evaluating and critiquing the messages we are receiving, but also intentionally cultivating communities that will empower us and help us experience love of self and others. This is REAL self-care. It's not just the physical accoutrement of hair, nails, makeup, and clothing (though all of that is good too!). We must do the work of holding space for ourselves and our sisters to take care of our mental, emotional, and spiritual well-being as well. It is through this kind of care for our whole selves that we experience freedom, find our voice, and soar.

But we can't do this work alone. This is where I implore those who love fat Black womxn to also embrace the messages of this book and be our allies in creating a new reality. You may love us as your child, partner, mother, auntie, sister, cousin, friend, parishioner, attorney, doctor, teacher, chef, and in many other ways that we show up in your lives—so, at the most fundamental level, I ask that you unapologetically demonstrate this love in all places and at all times. Then, go deeper.

Examine the way you talk to and about fat Black womxn. As Dr. Cox noted, we create and understand reality through our talk. When you constantly tell pejorative jokes about fat Black womxn, encourage your sister to diet, question your partner's choices to work out (or not), or tell your congregation that gluttony is sin, you are creating an environment that socializes fat Black girls and womxn to believe that they are not valued. You are normalizing fatphobia and healthism. Instead, I encourage you to talk about the wonderful and beautiful beings that fat Black womxn are, the ways they enrich your life, and the strength of their bodies. Further, I encourage you to critically examine the messages from the media about what "healthy" looks like, push back against the doctors who do not provide adequate treatment based on your daughter's size, and stand up for fat Black womxn when they are marginalized in everyday life. Normalize fat acceptance and the idea that people can be healthy at every size.

I am sure that embodying the lessons we have gleaned from Dr. Cox's work will not be easy. Fatphobia and other negative feelings and stereotypes about fat Black womxn have been ingrained into our society over centuries. But if we want to get free, we must do the work of confronting and decentering these narratives and their influence in our lives. It starts with doing the hard part—we must push our learning beyond knowing and understanding, and get to the point where we are actively using our collective voice to create new realities, adopt new ways of knowing ourselves, and develop new opportunities and communities that will allow fat Black womxn to thrive.

BIBLIOGRAPHY

Abdullah, T., J. Graham, A. Calloway, and L. M. West. 2017. "The Link between Experiences of Racism and Stress and Anxiety for Black Americans." Anxiety.org. March 16, 2017. www.anxiety .org/black-americans-how-to-cope-with-anxiety-and-racism.

African American Registry. n.d. "'Soul Food' a Brief History." African American Registry. Accessed February 27, 2020. https://aaregistry .org/story/soul-food-a-brief-history/.

Als, H. 2003. "Ghosts in the House: How Toni Morrison Fostered a Generation of Black Writers." *The New Yorker.* October 27, 2003. www.newyorker.com/magazine/2003/10/27/ghosts-in-the-house.

Asch, C. M. 2008. *The Senator and the Sharecropper: The Freedom Struggles of James O. Eastland and Fannie Lou Hamer.* Chapel Hill: University of North Carolina Press.

Association for Size Diversity and Health. n.d. "The Health at Every Size Approach." ASDAH. Accessed February 27, 2020. www .sizediversityandhealth.org/content.asp?id=76.

Bacon, L., and A. Severson. 2019. "Fat Is Not the Problem—Fat Stigma Is." *Scientific American.* July 8, 2019. https://blogs.scientific american.com/observations/fat-is-not-the-problem-fat-stigma-is/.

Baker, J. 2017. "Things No One Will Tell Fat Girls . . . So I Will." *HuffPost.* December 26, 2013; updated December 6, 2017. www .huffpost.com/entry/sex-relationships-fat-girls_b_4453713.

Battle, J., and C. Ashley. 2008. "Intersectionality, Heteronormativity, and Black Lesbian, Gay, Bisexual, and Transgender (LGBT) Families." *Black Women, Gender + Families* 2, no. 1: 1–24.

BBC News. 2007. "The Fattening Rooms of Calabar." BBC News. July 19, 2007. http://news.bbc.co.uk/2/hi/6904640.stm.

Beebe, J. 2018. "Black Women Suffer from Eating Disorders, Too." *The Daily Beast.* August 6, 2018. www.thedailybeast.com/black-women-suffer-from-eating-disorders-too.

Blain, C. 2019. "Mixed-Race, Non-Binary, Queer Fat Femme: How I Fail and Succeed in Finding Liberation." *The Body Is Not An Apology.* August 15, 2019. https://thebodyisnotanapology.com/magazine/fat-femm-my-f-you-to-traditional-beauty-standards-cicley-blain/.

Business Wire. 2019. "The U.S. Weight Loss & Diet Control Market." *Business Wire.* February 25, 2019. www.businesswire.com/news/home/20190225005455/en/72-Billion-Weight-Loss-Diet-Control-Market.

Butler, R. 2018. "Black Women and Their Oversexualized Bodies." *Bodylove: Gender, Sex, Culture, Folklore, and the Body.* March 27, 2018. https://sites.wp.odu.edu/bodylore/2018/03/27/black-women-and-their-oversexualized-bodies.

Center for Discovery. n.d. "Signs and Symptoms of Disordered Eating." Center for Discovery. Accessed February 27, 2020. https://centerfordiscovery.com/blog/signs-symptoms-disordered-eating/.

Cox, J. 2018. "Negotiating Identity and Taking Political Action in the Fat Liberation Movement." New Brunswick, NJ: RU Core Libraries.

Crawford, R. 1980. "Healthism and the Medicalization of Everyday Life." *International Journal of Health Services* 10, no. 3: 365–88.

Crenshaw, K. 1989. "Demarginalizing the Intersection of Race and Sex: A Black Feminist Critique of Antidiscrimination Doctrine, Feminist Theory and Antiracist Politics." *University of Chicago Legal Forum,* 139–67.

Crumpton, T. 2019. "Talking with Walela Nehanda about the Decolonization of Body Image through Cancer." Nylon. March 18, 2019. https://nylon.com/walela-nehanda-cancer-black-femme.

Democracy Now! 2017. "Disability Rights Activist Arrested for Protesting Trumpcare: We Won't Be Silent While You Kill Us." *Democracy*

Now! June 30, 2017. www.democracynow.org/2017/6/30/disability
_rights_activist_arrested_for_protesting.

Denise, C. 1999. "December 10, 1999: Shirley Hemphill Dies."
Black Then. December 11, 1999. https://blackthen.com/%E2
%80%8Bdecember-10-1999-shirley-hemphill-dies/.

DiAngelo, R., and M. E. Dyson. 2018. *White Fragility: Why It's So
Hard for White People to Talk about Racism.* Boston: Beacon
Press.

Dickman, L. 2017. "How Activist Crystal Newman Brought No-Diet
Day to the Kentucky Derby." *Wear Your Voice.* May 7, 2017.
https://wearyourvoicemag.com/body-politics/crystal-newman
-diet-day-kentucky-derby.

Dockray, H. 2017. "Trans and Non-binary Fitness Trainers Are
Building Tiny Empires—on Instagram." Mashable. December 27,
2017. https://mashable.com/2017/12/27/trans-non-binary-fitness
-celebrities-instagram/#B_SzeqxSsiqa.

Dolezal, L., and B. Lyons. 2017. "Health-Related Shame: An Affective
Determinant of Health?" *Medical Humanities* 43, no. 4: 257–63.

Durso, L. E., and G. J. Gates. 2012. "Serving Our Youth: Findings
from a National Survey of Service Providers Working with Lesbian, Gay, Bisexual, and Transgender Youth Who Are Homeless
or at Risk of Becoming Homeless." The Williams Institute with
True Colors Fund and The Palette Fund.

Emmer, C., M. Bosnjak, and J. Mata. 2020. "The Association between
Weight Stigma and Mental Health: A Meta-Analysis." *Obesity
Reviews* 21, no. 1: 1–13.

Epstein, R. B., J. Blake, and T. González. 2017. "Girlhood Interrupted:
The Erasure of Black Girls' Childhood." *SSRN*, June 27, 2017: 1–24.

Feeley-Harnik, G. 1995. "Religion and Food: An Anthropological
Perspective." *Journal of the American Academy of Religion* 63,
no. 3: 565–82.

Gaesser, G. 2009. "Is 'Permanent Weight Loss' an Oxymoron? The Statistics on Weight Loss and the National Weight Control Registry."

In *The Fat Studies Reader*, edited by E. Rothblum and S. Solovay, 37–41. New York: New York University Press.

Go Off Sis! 2019. "Black Women Talk Body Image in the Black Community." Refinery29. February 7, 2019. www.refinery29.com /en-us/black-women-body-image.

Gregory, S. 2010. *The Daniel Fast: Feed Your Soul, Strengthen Your Spirit, and Renew Your Body*. Grand Rapids, MI: Tyndale House.

Gwinup, G., R. Chelvam, and T. Steinberg. 1971. "Thickness of Subcutaneous Fat and Activity of Underlying Muscles." *Annals of Internal Medicine* 74, no. 3: 408–11.

Hampton, R. 2018. "The Fat Pride Movement Promotes Dignity, Not a 'Lifestyle.'" *Slate*. April 11, 2018. https://slate.com /human-interest/2018/04/fat-pride-movement-is-for-dignity-not -recruitment.html.

Harriot, M. 2019. "The 2019 Rules and Revisions for Black Thanksgiving." *The Root*. November 25, 2019. www.theroot.com/the -2019-rules-and-revisions-for-black-thanksgiving-1840024400.

Hayford, V. n.d. "The Humble History of Soul Food." Black Foodie. Accessed February 27, 2020. http://blackfoodie.co/the-humble -history-of-soul-food.

I Love Old School Music. 2018. "The Real Truth of Why Mabel King Got Fed Up & Suddenly Quit 'What's Happening.'" I Love Old School Music. June 6, 2018. www.iloveoldschoolmusic.com /the-real-truth-of-why-mabel-king-got-fed-up-suddenly-quit -whats-happening-2/.

Internet Movie Database. n.d. "The Wiz: Lena Horne: Glinda the Good." IMDb. Accessed February 27, 2020. www.imdb.com/title /tt0078504/characters/nm0395043.

Kaur, H. 2019. "At Least 22 Transgender People Have Been Killed This Year. But Numbers Don't Tell the Full Story." CNN. November 18, 2019. www.cnn.com/2019/11/18/us/transgender-killings -hrc-report-trnd/index.html.

Kaye, B. 2019. "Your Fatphobia Won't Make Me Dress Any Less Provocatively This Summer." Hello Giggles. June 18, 2019. https:// hellogiggles.com/beauty/fatphobia-summer-body/.

Khakh, A. 2019. "Shameless: Eating Disorders Are Not Just a White Feminists Issue." Flare. March 8, 2019. www.flare.com /identity/eating-disorder-awareness/?fbclid=IwAR1u1FICg -pWYyJT6k3iX_htEgmWfwRFsBaBLwGt2h_eEZqhwKhbG 5hFoeQ.

LeWine, H. 2012. "Diabetes Can Strike—Hard—Even When Weight Is Normal." *Harvard Health Blog.* August 8, 2012. www.health .harvard.edu/blog/diabetes-can-strike-hard-even-when-weight-is -normal-201208085121.

Love, H. 2018. "White Supremacy, Colonialism and Fatphobia Are Inherently Tied to Each Other." *Wear Your Voice.* November 21, 2018. https://wearyourvoicemag.com/body-politics/white -supremacy-colonialism-fatphobia.

Mays, V. M., S. D. Cochran, and N. W. Barnes. 2007. "Race, Race-Based Discrimination, and Health Outcomes among African Americans." *Annual Review of Psychology* 58: 201–25.

Melton, T. 2018. "Our Idea of Healthy Eating Excludes Other Cultures, and That's a Problem." *SELF.* July 31, 2018. www.self .com/story/our-idea-of-healthy-eating-excludes-other-cultures-and -thats-a-problem?fbclid=IwAR2A6t9XYYfSYCr8FAkn1nBNpeT UiRE9kla-er4nusL1U4hIsNLp0ctlcfc.

Merriam-Webster. "Merriam-Webster's Words of the Year 2019." 2019. Merriam-Webster. www.merriam-webster.com/words-at -play/word-of-the-year/they.

Meyer, R. 2018. "Dude, She's (Exactly 25 Percent) out of Your League." *The Atlantic.* August 10, 2018. www.theatlantic.com/science /archive/2018/08/online-dating-out-of-your-league/567083/.

Miles, M. 1995. "Religion and Food: The Case of Eating Disorders." *Journal of American Academy of Religion* LXIII, no. 3: 549–64.

Mills, K. 2007. "Fannie Lou Hamer: Civil Rights Activist." Mississippi History Now. http://mshistorynow.mdah.state.ms.us/articles/51 /fannie-lou-hamer-civil-rights-activist.

NBC. 1964. *Fannie Lou Hamer's Testimony at the 1964 Democratic Convention.* Film.

Norton, A. 2018. "'Southern' Diet Blamed for Black Americans' Health Woes." Medical Express. October 2, 2018. https://medicalxpress .com/news/2018-10-southern-diet-blamed-black-americans.html.

NPR. 2009. "Sapphire's Story: How 'Push' Became 'Precious.'" November 6, 2009. Interview.

Null, M. 2012. "Fat Stigma to Fat Acceptance: Fat Women's Size Acceptance as an Embodied Process." PhD diss., Purdue University. ProQuest.

Nuttall, F. Q. 2015. "Body Mass Index: Obesity, BMI, and Health. A Critical Review." *Nutrition Today* 50, no. 3: 117–28.

Parasecoli, F. 2015. "God's Diets: The Fat Body and the Bible as an Eating Guide in Evangelical Christianity." *Fat Studies* 4: 141–58.

Patton, T. O. 2006. "Hey Girl, Am I More Than My Hair?: African American Women and Their Struggles with Beauty, Body Image, and Hair." *NWSA Journal* 18: 24–51.

Phelan, S. M., D. J. Burgess, M. W. Yeazel, W. L. Hellerstedt, J. M. Griffin, and M. van Ryn. 2015. "Impact of Weight Bias and Stigma on Quality of Care." *Obesity Reviews* 16, no. 4: 319–26.

Rose, J. 2018. "The Black Community's Love for Homophobia." *Nubian Message.* November 29, 2018. www.thenubianmessage .com/2018/11/29/the-black-communitys-love-for-homophobia/.

Rubin, J. S. 2013. *The Maker's Diet: The 40-Day Health Experience That Will Change Your Life Forever.* Shippensburg, PA: Destiny Image.

Runfola, C. D., A. V. Holle, S. E. Trace, K. A. Brownley, S. M. Hofmeier, D. A. Gagne, et al. 2013. "Body Dissatisfaction in Women across the Lifespan: Results of the UNC-SELF and Gender and Body Image (GABI) Studies." *European Eating Disorders Review* 21, no. 1: 52–59.

Sadistic, F. B. 2019. "Why I'm No Longer Talking about Health." *Medium.* September 26, 2019. https://medium.com/@jervae/why -im-no-longer-talking-about-health-a7dbd042ba0f.

Sterry, R., and D. Sturtevant. 2015. "You Have the Right to Refuse to Be Weighed." Be Nourished. February 17, 2015. https://benourished .org/right-refuse-weighed/.

Strings, S. 2019. *Fearing the Black Body: The Racial Origins of Fat Phobia.* New York: New York University Press.

Stryker, K. 2016. "6 Ways I Was Taught to Be a Good Fatty (and Why I Stopped)." Everyday Feminism. April 16, 2016. https://everydayfeminism.com/2016/04/taught-to-be-good-fatty/.

Taylor, J. Y., C. H. Caldwell, R. E. Baser, N. Faison, and J. S. Jackson. 2007. "Prevalence of Eating Disorders among Blacks in the National Survey of American Life." *International Journal of Eating Disorders* 40 (Suppl.): S10–S14.

Taylor, K. 2016. *From #BlackLivesMatter to Black Liberation.* Chicago: Haymarket Books.

Turner, G. n.d. "Disease Does Not Discriminate, but U.S. Public Health Does." MPH Online. Accessed February 27, 2020. www.mphonline.org/racism-public-health/.

West, C. M. 2008. "Mammy, Jezebel, Sapphire, and Their Homegirls: Developing an 'Oppositional Gaze' toward the Images of Black Women." In *Lectures on the Psychology of Women,* edited by J. C. Chrisler, C. Golden, and P. D. Rozee, 286–99. New York: McGraw-Hill.

Williams, A. A. 2017. "Fat People of Color: Emergent Intersectional Discourse Online." *Social Sciences* 6, no. 1: 1–16.

Williams, O., and E. Annandale. 2019. "Weight Bias Internalization as an Embodied Process: Understanding How Obesity Stigma Gets under the Skin." *Frontiers in Health Psychology* 10: 953.

Yeboah, S. 2019. "I Found Out the Guy I Was Dating Did It for a Dare. Here's What Happened Next." Refinery29. February 8, 2019. www.refinery29.com/en-gb/pull-a-pig-dating-pranks.

Zidenberg, A. M., B. Sparks, L. Harkins, and S. K. Lidstone. 2019. "Tipping the Scales: Effects of Gender, Rape Myth Acceptance, and Anti-Fat Attitudes on Judgments of Sexual Coercion Scenarios." *Journal of Interpersonal Violence,* August 2019: 1–27.

ACKNOWLEDGMENTS

I do not think I have the time or the pages to thank everyone who has played a part in me writing this book! I am almost hesitant to name names, as I know I will forget to name someone and drown in shame when I realize it. Know that even if your name is not mentioned specifically here, if we have ever held conversation about these matters, you are not forgotten. I am just forgetful.

To my publisher:

I am deeply appreciative and humbled for being asked to write my story and that of others by North Atlantic Books. Special thanks to Shayna Keyles, who assisted in keeping me on track with content and deadlines throughout this ordeal.

To my family:

Words cannot express my gratitude, but I'll try. To my mom, thank you for being there and advocating on my behalf when no one else did. Your strength has been a faithful reminder of what rests on the inside of me. If you can make it through what you have and still smile, so can I. To my sisters, Dawn and April, thank you for your support! Life can be hard at times, but it's always great to have those whom you can laugh with, cry with, and get the words wrong to popular songs with along the way. Life would be a bit duller without you both. I'd probably have more snacks, but definitely duller. To my Aunt Pearl and Grandmom Bert, you laid quite the foundation! I have not forgotten about you. I see you in all I do. I'm grateful for all you have instilled in me. To my dad, life is not the same without you here, but I hear you, your instructions, and your encouragements through every dream you show up in. I'm grateful for your presence. I'm also grateful for your love. To all the other family members who have encouraged me to be myself and live my best life, I appreciate you! For all those who cheered me on when I used to dance to MC Hammer and Janet Jackson videos, I thank you! For those who could see my potential and believed in me more than I believed in myself, I love y'all! Y'all are written in the crevices of my lived experiences. The world has been a bit brighter for me because of you.

To my friends:

What is one to say about the "family" you choose! Fanny Ramirez, you are one of my biggest supporters, and I count it an honor to be called your friend. Never stop shining. It brings life to those around you. Amana Kazakasi, girl! I messed around and wrote a BOOK! Thank you for being my getaway from the hustle and bustle of life. Thank you for all the congratulatory messages and jokes about research and all its drama! Your silliness has kept me sane. To my internet bestie, Marlena Johnson, you are such a light! Grateful for the memes and jokes, and the chats and phone conversations on how to get our lives together. Seeing you win lets me know the future will be okay. To my real-life besties, it has been quite a journey! Helena Tisinger, thank you for checking in and cheering me on. Little things like this let me know that friendship can last despite distance. To Bunmi Alo, thank you for insisting I accept the opportunity to write this. I'm glad I listened to your advice. THIS TIME you were right. . . .

To the fat Black community:

My people, we are and will always be more than enough! I love you all to pieces. I hope I have done our stories some justice in this writing. I hope that this will be something you can share with the next generation of excellent human beings coming up under your wings.

To mentors, teachers, and inspirations:

To the fat-positive organizations ASDAH and NAAFA, I'm grateful for a documented history that can tell the stories of those who have come before us. Thank you for your commitment to advocacy and antiracism in more recent times. I'm grateful to have been present for some of your growth. Thank you for the resources shared and the movement toward liberation. To Christy Harrison, thank you for your insight and giving me a voice through your platform to share my story. To the online space Magical Fat Black Femmes and founder Brandi Wharton, I see the lives you save daily. It is an honor being welcomed, and I thank you for creating the space where magic happens. To Bernadette Gailliard-Mayabi, advisor! Thank you for your insight and guidance through all my research and rants as I wrote what I didn't know at the time would be a preface for this book. To those who published works before me, thank you for being my teachers. I would've never learned without you. For those who dare to be different and "let it all hang out," whether that be in body or personality, thank you for inspiring me to do the same.

To everyone else:

If you have ever written or shared a story that spoke out against racism and fat hatred, if you have ever encouraged me or seen me as more than my body, I thank you! We all fight different battles, and I am grateful that you stood with me as I fought mine. Much love and well wishes to all the hands that this book might touch.

INDEX

defense, fending off fat attitudes,
8–9
Devoe, Y Falami, 110
diabetes
A1c test for, 65
author's Gram diagnosed with, 5
health complications related to
weight, 14–15
diet. *See* food/diet
dignity, fat acceptance as tool
of, 51
disability rights, partnering with
fat activism, 77
disdain, for fat people asserting
body acceptance, 60
doctors
anger directed towards, 49
fat activism and, 77
impact of recommendations
relative to weight, 38–41
Dodson, Tiana, 83, 99
"Dreams and Schemes" fund, 106
dress. *See* clothing
drug addiction, stereotypal
assumptions, 12

E

earnings/income, cost of weight
stigma, 9–10
eating disorders
Black women suffering from, 72
Christianity and, 28
dieting and, 65–66
weight loss programs
impacting, 12
educators, role in changing the
world, 110–111
E-K Daufin & Associates, 111
*Eloquent Rage: A Black Feminist
Discovers Her Superpower*
(Cooper), 107

emotions
cost of weight stigma, 9
defending against fat
prejudices, 9
unpacking stigmas and
biases, 52
empathy, not a justification for
abuse, 126
employment, cost of weight
stigma, 9–10
empowerment
fat acceptance as tool of, 51
refusing rejection, 49
encouragement, finding in Black
fat family, 93
entertainment, options for Black
fat adults, 94
eShakti brand, of clothing, 88–89
Evans, Stacie, 107
evil, Black culture and religion
and, 25–26
exercise
athleticism/fitness/movement,
110
cost of, 68
dizzy spells, 67
fatphobia at gyms, 79
getting results, 64–67
value of weight loss industry, 71

F

Facebook, 60
family. *See also* Black fat family
author's acknowledgments,
145–146
author's experience of being
uprooted and relocating in
childhood, xviii–xxi
author's recollection of, xv–xviii
coming home in Dakar,
114–115

femmes/femininity. *See also* MFBF
(Magical Fat Black Femmes)
Black culture and religion
and, 24
Fat White Women in Black
culture aesthetics, 61–62
objectification of body, 7–8
resistance groups, 81
sexual identity prejudices, 11–12
fetishes, regarding fat women, 52
fighting back. *See also* activism
doing the work, 83–84
standing up to bullying, 76
financial mobility, U.S.
propaganda about need for, 118
fitness factory, 68
"food pyramid," limitations and
racial bias in, 72
food/diet
activism, 82
in Black culture, 31–33
breaking free of healthism,
70–71
chefs as healers, 110
childhood experience of author,
xxiii
Christianity and, 28–30
combining with exercise,
66–67
cost of dieting, 68
diet culture based on White
supremacy, 15
eating disorders and, 65–66
healthism and, 40
intuitive eating, 72–73
related to Black churches, 34–36
self-control and, 30
three meals a day rule, 72–73
freedom, by dealing with own shit,
122–123
Freedom Farm Cooperative, 106

Fresh Out the Cocoon podcast
activism, 83
common experience of guests
on, 20
implementing and common
themes in, 98
launching as form of activism,
81
learning lessons from sisters,
98–100
"paying it forward" as the why
behind activism, 100–101
trolls confronting author, 60
t-shirt design, 96
"What's so hard about learning
people?," 131–132
friends/friendship
author's acknowledgments, 146
cost of weight stigma, 9
fat friend roles, 8–9

G

Gailliard-Mayabi, Dr. Bernadette,
110, 131–135, 147
gaslighting
communicative tactics, 60
cost of choosing sides, 63
related to being fat, 76
Gay, Roxane, 107
gender
activism of Makia Green, 106
fighting against inequality, 129
prejudices and danger to
LGBTQ+ community, 10–11
size, gender, race in triple
consciousness of Black
women, 127, 129
genetics, fatness and, 36
Ghana, 114
Gilliam, Amanda, 66, 110
Gilmore, Geneieve, 109

ABOUT THE AUTHOR

*J*oy Arlene Renee Cox is an ordinary person who has been given an ordinary opportunity to share stories about people much more fabulous than herself. She is a Philadelphia native, born on the blessed thirty-first day of December. Joy is a claircognizant Capricorn that thrives through connection and love, rooting for the underdogs in life to take their rightful place as overcomers. She is also a doctor; she received her PhD from Rutgers University–New Brunswick in 2018. Her field of work is centered on fatness, identity, and social change.

Reflective of the name she bears, Joy has the cheeks to outsmile her detractors. Reflective of her work in print, she has the research to back up her claims. While the spotlight has never been a position she'd prefer to stand in, Joy does believe in speaking up and advocating for what's right. She is the host of the pro-fat, pro-Black podcast *Fresh Out the Cocoon* and has been featured in articles by the *Huffington Post* and *SELF* magazine. Joy has also been on several podcasts, such as *Positive Nutrition* with Paige Smathers and *Food Psych* with Christy Harrison. Dr. Cox is simply a conduit through which love, wisdom, and justice flow. Her pride is in her people and her values. Her strength is in her disposition and her intuition.

About North Atlantic Books

North Atlantic Books (NAB) is an independent, nonprofit publisher committed to a bold exploration of the relationships between mind, body, spirit, and nature. Founded in 1974, NAB aims to nurture a holistic view of the arts, sciences, humanities, and healing. To make a donation or to learn more about our books, authors, events, and newsletter, please visit www.northatlanticbooks.com.

North Atlantic Books is the publishing arm of the Society for the Study of Native Arts and Sciences, a 501(c)(3) nonprofit educational organization that promotes cross-cultural perspectives linking scientific, social, and artistic fields. To learn how you can support us, please visit our website.